8 Great Dates for Dads & Daughters

Talking with Your Daughter About
Understanding
Boys

8 Great Dates for Dads & Daughters

Talking with Your Daughter About

Understanding Boys

Bob and Dannah Gresh

With Jarrod Sechler and Suzanna D'Souza

HARVEST HOUSE PUBLISHERS
EUGENE, OREGON

Cover by www.DesignbyJulia.com, Colorado

Cover photos © Joe Belanger, kazoka, inxti / Shutterstock

Interior design by Harvest House Publishers, Oregon and www.DesignbyJulia.com, Colorado

Interior photos: p.45: Sechler family, used by permission; pp. 66, 84, 165, courtesy Wikimedia Commons

Interior icons and illustrations: Julia Ryan; others by Shutterstock.com

SECRET KEEPER GIRL is a registered trademark of Dannah Gresh.

TALKING WITH YOUR DAUGHTER ABOUT UNDERSTANDING BOYS
8 Great Dates for Dads and Daughters series
Copyright © 2014 by Dannah Gresh
Published by Harvest House Publishers
Eugene, Oregon 97402
www.harvesthousepublishers.com

Library of Congress Cataloging-in-Publication Data
    Gresh, Bob.
    Talking with your daughter about understanding boys / Bob and Dannah Gresh
        pages cm. — (8 great dates for dads and daughters)
    ISBN 978-0-7369-5534-8 (pbk.)
    ISBN 978-0-7369-5535-5 (eBook)
    1. Fathers and daughters—Religious aspects—Christianity. 2. Girls—Religious life. 3. Boys.
    I. Title.
    BV4529.17.G74 2014
    248.8'421—dc23
                                                            2013031085

14 15 16 17 18 19 20 21 22 / VP-JH / 10 9 8 7 6 5 4 3 2 1

To five of my favorite fathers…
Jarrod Sechler
Dave Anderson
Pat Sullivan
Jim Burtoft
Troy VanLiere
… five guys I trust to call me a knucklehead when I act like one
(one for each knuckle).
Watching their lives has made me a better father.

And to Dannah's dad and my dad,
who love us like crazy.

—Bob

Thank You

This book was a team effort. In the history of all Gresh books, none have ever taken so many people to pull it together. We were writing a book for dads that also needed to appeal to their daughters but would likely be bought by their wives. Need we say more? We've done a lot of rewrites to get this…right.

Terry Glaspey, LaRae Weikert, and Barb Sherrill from Harvest House Publishers saw the ministry value of creating an 8 Great Dates book for dads and daughters. (Even though we all know moms buy more books.) They have a true heart for ministry and we love 'em.

Jarrod Sechler joined with Bob for long brainstorming sessions and wrote some of the content. (You'll hear from Jarrod personally in the pages ahead.) Another of Bob's friends, Jim Burtoft, gave us great ideas and great feedback. They are both true friends to me (Bob) and my family. They carry the load with me when it is heavy, and they are two of the best dads I know.

Suzanna D'Souza was the editor for this project and also created a lot of the content. She kept us thinking like girls! (And with three dads working on the project, she was really outnumbered.) She was patient and excellent in all ways.

WHAT'S IN THIS BOOK

Part 3:
Other Great Stuff

A Note from Bob

Caution!

As commentator Bill O'Reilly would say, "Caution—you're about to enter the no-spin zone."

It's amazing how political correctness intrudes into every aspect of our lives. It's even politically incorrect in "enlightened" circles to identify someone by such a limiting factor as *male* or *female*. Those in such circles see many more options.

We don't.

This book is written for dads and daughters. At times, it assumes that Mom and Dad are married. We believe that it's ideal (and biblical) for a man to marry one woman, raise kids, and be married lifelong.

We also know that we don't live in an ideal world. Family structures are so splintered today that we can't address all of them, and so we chose the father of the intact family to be the assumed reader of this book.

We have a huge heart for single moms, single dads, and splintered families. My heart breaks over parents who desperately need a godly male or female role model for their kids. (We have included a special section in this book for single moms.)

Customize the pronouns for your own situation, take what applies, and disregard stuff that doesn't match your family.

The role of women in the church and at home is a hot topic—and a complex one. Some women are girly-girls and some are tomboys, which makes things even more complicated. So...

After much discussion (and rewriting) we decided that our

9

model for womanhood was the mom of Proverbs 31. She was a mix of everything. (Her husband married well. So did I.)

Now, with that attempt to explain our approach in advance, let's go on some adventures together. Read on!

Bob

How This Works

by Bob

We're dads.

We're different.

We have different parts. We have different styles than women.

Statistically, we don't read as much—80 percent of Christian books are for women and are read by women.

I've made this book as easy to use as possible because your life is packed full of stuff, and I don't want to add any more weight (or aggravation) than necessary.

For years, moms have been using the Secret Keeper Girl 8 Great Dates books to grow closer to their daughters. Almost all of those books point out that the relationship a dad has with his daughter informs how she responds to boys. (I recently cheered on a fellow dad, Dr. Thomas White, the president of Cedarville University. He said this publicly: "Mess with me, that's bad. Mess with my wife, that's really going to be bad for you. Mess with my daughter—that's me being called to prison ministry from the inside!" Of course he was joking...sort of.) Here's a quick look at what's going to happen in the pages to come.

Part 1: Dads Matter–No Matter What the World Says.

This is an introductory welcome to the idea of "dating" your daughter. We'll give you ideas on how to spend time with your girl while teaching her things she should know. Skim these chapters if you want. Don't skip them.

Part 2: 8 Great Dates. Check them out and you'll see that they're really easy to use. Each date has simple plans to do activities that will help you talk to your girl. **Look, let's admit it's sometimes awkward to keep the conversation going—** these dates will fix that.

Part 3: Other Great Stuff. This section is used on an as-needed basis. Other than the "Talk with Dad" pullouts for your daughter, you may not need much of it at all. But everything is explained as you get to it.

I think you'll enjoy this. Step up. Do it right. You'll make memories for a lifetime.

Now I'll introduce Dannah. She's been working with and researching girls for 15 years, and she's literally written the books on how they tick. Read the preface and the following chapters. You'll see why these years are the most important ones of your daughter's life. This short time will shape her values forever.

Bob

A Dad's Hug

by Dannah

It was one of the saddest days of my life.

Bob and I had worn each other out. After attempts at counseling, we were still unyielded to the healing power of Christ. With the help of two pastors and a counselor who loved us and wanted to see us go the distance, **we had decided to separate for three weeks.** [1]

I would go to my parents' home in Pennsylvania.

He would stay at our home in Missouri.

I started my drive while the stormy morning was still dark—my two precious kids in the backseat. Tears blinded my eyes. The windshield wipers worked overtime. The weather seemed to be a picture of my marriage. I could hardly bear to wait this storm out. Tractor-trailers with the word "swift" seemed to litter the highway, and I made them my prayer.

Please, Lord, let this three weeks go by swiftly.

I felt like I couldn't breathe, but I wanted to make it in time, so I kept driving. In a matter of hours, my daddy would be shooting off a masterpiece that would paint the night sky with color. There would be no missing what had been deemed one of America's ten largest fireworks displays. [2] The speed limit was frustrating me as I headed toward the Great American Fourth of July Fireworks Festival in my Pennsylvania hometown.

Finally, as dusk invited 200,000 eager tailgaters to pull out their lawn chairs and blankets, my white minivan pulled into the VIP parking lot. The crowd was thick. And it was way before cell phones. How would I find my parents? I headed to the VIP

tent and hoped one of them would be nearby. If I timed it just right I would see my mom hostessing all of the community leaders, but getting to see my dad before the show was probably an impossible dream. They both knew why I was coming.

Mom was there, as I'd hoped. My kids wasted no time in climbing all over her, and she was happy to hand her walkie-talkie and hostessing title over to her assistant so she could wear her "Grammy" hat. But not before giving me a hug, and then a job—because she could see I was about to lose it. I needed to stay busy.

The hot dogs I cooked that night may have looked a little like charcoal when I was finished. My mind kept wandering as I looked into the distance, hoping my dad might stop by the tent.

I still remember what he was wearing when I saw him. A yellow Land's End windbreaker cut the evening chill. He walked toward me with purpose and enveloped me in his arms.

Then, I cried.

And I'm crying now as I write about it.

What safety was in that hug! I knew then that it was going to be all right. My daddy's hug fueled me with hope.

ABOUT DAD'S HUG

According to Dr. Meg Meeker, a father's degree of physical affection toward his daughter is directly related to her self-esteem.[3] Hug her. Often. And long.

PART 1

Dads Matter—No Matter What the World Says

Dads Run Deep

by Dannah

You probably picked up this book with the sole intention of helping your little girl grow closer to you. But I'm praying it also helps you come to terms with your feelings about *having* a Father.

Maybe your relationship with your own dad has been phenomenal and the two of you are especially close. Or maybe it's nonexistent and the only thing the two of you have in common is DNA. Maybe dad was your biggest fan at soccer practices. Or maybe he filled your college fund but never filled your love tank. Maybe you never even knew your biological father. Or maybe you knew him well and you've had to grieve the painful loss of a best friend.

Good, bad, or distant—dads run deep.

Deeper than we might think.

An article published by the *Journal for the Scientific Study of Religion* discovered a strong correlation between a child's image of her parents—specifically her father—and her perception of God. [4] In fact, the correlation was even stronger for girls than it was for boys.

Which means that if a little girl sees her father as powerful and nurturing, then she'll easily come to terms with a God who is omnipotent but still cares for the sparrows. [5] Conversely, if a little girl sees her father as distant—or if she doesn't see her father at all—then it'll be difficult for her to embrace this idea of a God who calls himself Emmanuel, God *with* her.

Some of us are already pretty familiar with the God of Scripture who calls himself our Father. Our *Abba*. Literally meaning "daddy" or papa. See, in America, a baby begins to speak between 14 and 18 months and her first word is usually *da—da, da, daddy*. But a Jewish baby in first-century Palestine at the same age would have begun to say *ab—ab, ab, Abba*.

According to the great, dearly loved and much missed Brennan Manning, "Jesus is saying we may address the infinite, transcendent, almighty God with the intimacy, familiarity, and unshaken trust that a sixteen-month-old baby has sitting on his father's lap—*da, da, daddy*." [6]

Do you trust him like that?

He is a good Father. Even if yours wasn't.

TO SINGLE PARENTS

Right up front, Bob and I want to acknowledge that you might be doing your parenting on your own. This makes the book and the dates all that more important. The special challenges of single parenting include helping your children have a healthy view of how men and women were designed to be a reflection of God's image and to form families. We want to encourage the single dads to plow through this with passion! For single moms, we have a special section near the end of the book with advice. Check it out on page 135.

Bob is not perfect. Neither am I. And we've chosen to begin this book with a glimpse into our brokenness for a reason. We've picked up far too many books on parenting or marriage and felt defeated by the perfection in the pages. Devotions every morning during a full breakfast? Never did it! A family night every week? Meant well, but just couldn't seem to be that consistent!

Praying for our children as we tucked them into bed? Sometimes we just didn't have the energy for much more than a rote, meaningless prayer. Oh, we did a lot of things right, and we prayed with and for our kids and taught them to love God, but we aren't the poster parents for all things Christian.

We are the poster family for a God who repairs. In fact, one of our favorite verses is Psalm 127:1:

> *"Unless the LORD builds the house, those who build it labor in vain. Unless the LORD watches over the city, the watchman stays awake in vain."*

One day I was studying this verse and learned that the Hebrew word for "builds" in it means "to make and to repair." I don't know about yours, but the Gresh house has needed a lot of building and a lot of repairs. I praise my precious Lord, who has done more renovations on these two parents' hearts than my uncle who owns a remodeling business has to homes. Bob and Dannah Gresh were certainly two "fixer-uppers"!

Need a little fixing up? You've come to the right place.

Stop for a moment and ask the Holy Spirit to make your heart soft and tender to the truth and encouragement in the pages ahead. After all, how does a parent connect their daughter to God as a Father—unless *you* know Him in that way too?

Invest time in thinking of God as your heavenly Father as you approach these dates.

> *"[The Spirit which] you have now received [is] not a spirit of slavery to put you once more in bondage to fear, but you have received the Spirit of adoption…in [the bliss of] which we cry, Abba!…Father!'*

> *Romans 8:15* AMP, *brackets in original*

by Dannah

One of Bob's most interesting moments as a dad happened when Lexi was about 17. He found her boyfriend in the loft leading to her bedroom. Alex is a good and godly boy (but Bob says none of them seem really that good or that godly when it's your daughter they have their eyes on). He was up there innocently playing his ukulele in the loft.

"Alex, are you in Lexi's bedroom?" Bob sternly asked.

"Yes," came the response.

"Why?" he asked (more sternly).

No answer. But Bob soon saw him padding down the stairs in his socks with a frightened look on his face. "Sorry, Mr. Gresh. I wasn't in her bedroom."

By this point I think Alex may have been terrified. As Bob tells the story, he—Bob—went into our bedroom for a moment. When he returned, Alex was sitting in a chair in the living room.

"Didn't we talk about the rules of our house?" Bob questioned. "Was I unclear? Did you think I was kidding? I wasn't!"

Alex scooted further back into the chair. Bob went out of the room for a minute and then came back.

"Why are you still here?" Bob asked calmly. "Get out of my house!"

Alex did.

Point made.

Bob and I really like Alex and like spending time with him, but Bob makes no bones about maintaining our boundaries. It's not a dad's job to be your daughter's friend. Your first job, Dad, is to protect your daughter.

We call that story one of Bob's "Wolf Dad" moments. Wolves teach their young to hunt and be strong and provide for themselves. They help their wolf pups take risks and learn to survive and thrive in life. And they aren't afraid to snarl at danger or even at their own pups if they are out of line. Wolf dads do the same. They are "dangerous." And protective at the same time. (But that's a whole other book.)

Look—it's okay to be dangerous and safe and scary and scared and loud and quiet and anything else necessary for the good of your family and the world you live in. And the fact is, you and your daughter live in a world of boys. Understanding them is important. (Since you are one, you probably understand more than you'd like; but your daughter…she doesn't have a clue!)

Chances are that boys might soon begin to pursue your daughter. Then again, in today's culture it's just as likely that *your* little girl might be doing the pursuing. In a few short decades the wind has changed. Men have been terribly emasculated, while we girls have been told we're superior. From the bestselling books for women to the commercials that make men the butt of every joke, the feminist movement has done much to destroy the strength of men. Your daughter's been told often that she should go after what she wants and do it aggressively.

The New York Times published an article titled "She's Got to Be a Macho Girl" that offered a commentary on this shift: "Whether they are influenced by the trickle-down effects of feminism, which has taught girls to be assertive in all areas of life, or have internalized the images of sexually powerful women in popular culture, American girls are more daring than ever."[7] Which is why 17-year-old Sarah thinks asking a guy out is normal. "No one is a stay-at-home mom anymore," she said. "Women don't have to wear skirts. We are empowered and we can do whatever we want."[8]

And that empowerment—well, "they apply it to pursuing boys."[9] And that's where our concern comes in: everything pressed upon our girls is so sexual. Although there's nothing wrong with encouraging girls to excel, pursue their dreams, and be strong women, the danger lies in what Dennis Rainey calls "a *lifestyle of aggression*—doing whatever it takes to get what they want, no matter who they hurt—especially using their sexuality to exert power over men."[10]

Using her sexuality to exert power over men? She's only nine!

■ Exactly.

And she's already deciding what she believes about boys, girls, and how they're supposed to interact. Your daughter is exposed *daily* to a shocking number of sexual images and references that question gender and sexual roles. **The American Psychological Association estimates she'll see 14,000 annually as a teen.** That's roughly 38 times a day that your daughter will be told her value lies in being overtly sexual.[11] As adults, you and I can tune them out and exercise discernment. (Okay…I can't *always* tune those sexual messages out and exercise discernment as a fully grown woman. Can you? Neither can the boys your daughter is going to share her teen years with. Think about that for a minute. Now, stop thinking about it. Breathe deeply. Let's move on.)

Here's the thing—your daughter's brain is more like a sponge than a filter. Her eyes and ears soak in all the messages about womanhood image by image and message by message. She's learning by example what a woman is supposed to become.

CAN GIRLS BE GROWING UP TOO FAST?

The findings of a two-year study by an APA task force state that clothing that makes girls appear older—and the associated marketing efforts—are linked to eating disorders, low self-esteem, and depression. Ironically, this early sexualization presented to young girls also has "negative consequences on girls' ability to develop healthy sexuality."[12]

Moms need to teach their girls what it *really* means to be a woman. But it's extremely important that Dad is involved too. Why? Because a father generally has as much or *even more* impact than a mom on many aspects of his daughter's life, particularly when it comes to the way she approaches men.[13] This makes sense since Dad is, by far, the most significant male figure in her life.

Here are a few things from my research about the unique struggles girls face, which I have tried to download into Bob's brain. He thought you should get the data too.

Boy-Craziness

Hardly any of you men fell in "love" when you were in preschool, but for girls this can be somewhat normal. Three-year-old Cody became an overnight YouTube sensation after shedding more than a few tears because of her love for Justin Bieber. Boy-craziness hits earlier than ever these days! Almost half of tweens say they have or have had a boyfriend–girlfriend relationship. Which means that even if your daughter isn't boy-crazy, her friends probably are.

But here's the shocking part of that statistic. **While most tweens thought a "boyfriend-girlfriend relationship" meant "holding hands" or saying "I like you," nearly 30 percent thought it meant having oral sex or sexual**

intercourse! [14] If that weren't bad enough, after analyzing the top factors that place a girl at risk for sexual activity as a teen, the Medical Institute for Sexual Health concluded that a key predictor is having a boyfriend for six months or longer. [15] A boyfriend might seem "cute" when she's eight, but it sets her up for serial dating and puts both her heart and body at risk.

According to psychologists from the University of St. Andrews, girls with absent or uninvolved fathers are at risk for an earlier sexual debut and a greater number of sexual partners. [16] Fatherlessness is also unequivocally connected to teen pregnancy. [17]

CLICK HERE! :

Strong Fathers, Strong Daughters by Dr. Meg Meeker. Ever wish your daughter came with an instruction manual? This book is the next best thing! For dads with girls of all ages, Meeker divulges ten practical secrets to help your daughter become a strong, confident woman.

The good news is that when dad *is* involved, his presence becomes the crucial protective factor against early sexual outcomes, even when other risk factors are present. [18] A longitudinal study conducted with the National Institute of Child Health and Development found that regardless of socioeconomic status, race, nationality, personality, history, upbringing, stress, and even exposure to dysfunctional marriages, the father factor remained the fundamental link. [19]

In other words, a dad trumps all that.

"Beauty Knows No Pain"...Yeah, Right!

I'll admit I'd like to shed a few pounds. And I've even cried about it, though a little less as I mature. Bob would like to lose

some weight, too. He doesn't cry. So…he doesn't get it when he watches our beautiful girls struggle too. I do.

It's been shown that 80 percent of American women are dissatisfied with their appearance.[20] My guess is the other 20 percent were just having a good hair day when the survey was taken. Ever since Eve bought into the serpent's deceitful sales pitch, girls have been genetically predisposed to believe lies, especially about beauty. **You know your daughter is fearfully and wonderfully made (and you're not a bit biased), but your little girl looks in the mirror and wonders.**

According to the National Eating Disorders Association, 46 percent of girls ages 9 to 11 admit to having gone on a diet. (Again, even if your daughter hasn't, her friends probably have.) Among 10-year-olds, 81 percent are terrified of being "fat"—even though many of them are underweight. That obsession with appearances can easily escalate into a full-fledged eating disorder. Anorexia affects 1 out of every 100 girls, sometimes girls as young as 6. A dad may not be able to empathize with the craze to be skinny, but researchers adamantly maintain that he plays a critical role in both preventing eating disorders and healing his daughter if one takes root.[21]

When a dad speaks Truth, it's louder than the ugliest beauty lie. It's time to get started.

> *"Which of you, if your son asks for bread, will give him a stone? Or if he asks for a fish, will give him a snake? If you, then, though you are evil, know how to give good gifts to your children, how much more will your Father in heaven give good gifts to those who ask him!"*
>
> Jesus, in Matthew 7:9-11

by Bob

For years, I've wanted to take the successful concept of Dannah's *8 Great Dates for Moms and Daughters* and give dads the opportunity to get involved. What better topic for a dad to tackle than that of understanding guys and how girls relate to them?

As a guy with attention deficit disorder—*squirrel!*—it's sometimes hard for me to focus on one thing for a while, but I sure do have a lot of ideas. You'll find a lot of them in this book. I've designed them so they're easy—not girly and embarrassing—and so they can take as little or as much preparation time as you want.

⟿ SQUIRREL!

If you've seen the movie UP with your daughter, then you've met Dug the dog, who is easily distracted by squirrels. Having ADD, I'm the human counterpart. On occasion you'll see a Squirrel! comment that might seem random, but think hard. Really hard. It probably fits somehow!

Look, I'll admit it straight up. Many times I have the best of intentions beforehand, but when the date with my daughter or a commitment comes along, I sometimes find myself

scrambling to do it right. Don't take the easy route through all of the dates, but don't put too much pressure on yourself either. The most important thing for you to achieve is some "quantity" time with your daughter. I know "they" say that quality is more important than quantity, but don't kid yourself. "They" probably have bratty or lonely kids. Both quality and quantity count. Your daughter needs great quality time with you and a lot of it.

MOM–

If you're reading this, back away from the book.
Your husband can handle this. He really can.

These dates with your daughter will help her explore God's truth about her relationship with her heavenly Father, about love and marriage, and about boys. (Yes, boys who are likely to act just like you and I did. Scary.)

Don't worry about doing or saying everything right. (You won't.) Just be willing to listen to and talk with her. That's huge in a little girl's heart.

Each date lasts about an hour and a half, but it will fly by quickly. Don't forget to take a few pictures or videos along the way. (You'll earn big points for this later.) You can do these dates weekly or just spread them out and do them as you can schedule them into your life.

What You'll Find in This Book

Each date has a different topic and activity, but each of them from start to finish will have the same components:

Step 1: Prep Talk

This is just you and me hashing it out as dads, because sometimes you need a little prep talk before you walk into girl territory. On occasion I've asked my writing partner Jarrod Sechler or Dannah to write these. No matter who brings the prep talk, it's going to help you have an understanding of the *why* of what you're doing.

Step 2: SKG Radio for Your Ride to the Challenge

What guy doesn't like a little technology? We think that a little bit of "SKG Radio" is just what you need to kick off each date. Dannah and I have recorded some short conversations, stories, and challenges for you to play as you commence each date. You'll find the free, downloadable MP3's on the SKG website at www.secretkeepergirl.com.

Step 3: Dad-Daughter Challenge

The core of each of the 8 Great Dates is a Challenge Activity. (Think treasure hunts, wilderness hikes, and stargazing adventures.) You can modify them as much as you like, and there are "budget-crunching" ideas in case you need them. Each activity sets you up to have an important conversation about understanding boys…and girls…and how they interact. Here's a brief look at each date:

Date #1:
Mission Possible!

Challenge activity: Adventure Pranking 101
Key verse: Jeremiah 29:11
Objective: To begin to understand boys as
a part of God's good plan
Materials needed: Supplies for your favorite
practical joke, or one of mine

Date #2:
Sugar and Spice and Everything Nice

Challenge activity: Recipe for Success
Key verses: Proverbs chapter 31
Objective: To begin to understand what it
means to be a girl
Materials needed: Baking ingredients,
an empty kitchen

Date #3:
As You Wish

Challenge activity: Movie Night
Key verses: 1 Corinthians 13:4-8
Objective: To discover the difference between
true love and counterfeit love
Materials needed: *The Princess Bride* movie,
movie-watching munchables

Date #4:
Sticks and Stones (or the "Italian Job")

Challenge activity: A Wilderness Adventure Hike
Key verses: Psalm 62:5-6
Objective: To learn to believe that her value
comes from God, not a boy
Materials needed: Hiking boots, water bottle,
snacks, and a bag to collect several rocks

PREP FOR LIFE

Dads, we have the awesome privilege of helping to prepare
our daughters for life. Our Prep for Life sections—one for
each date—include bonus activities that tie in to what you're
doing on the date. You might teach your daughter to leave
a tip, hang a picture, or flip burgers on the grill. The activities
are easy and kids love them. Do as many as you can. You can
even add your own.

Date #5:
Natural Treasure

Challenge activity: A Treasure Hunt
Key verse: Proverbs 31:10
Objective: To discover that she is a treasure and
should expect to be treated as one
Materials needed: Clues for the hunt, and a treasure—
a piece of jewelry (can be simple and inexpensive,
but make it special)

Date #6:
How Does Your Garden Grow?

Challenge activity: Plant Something
Key verses: Psalm 1:1-3
Objective: To grow by feeding herself with God's Word
Materials needed: Seeds or a plant, a place to
plant it or them

Date #7:
Star Track—The Final Frontier

Challenge activity: Stargazing
Key verse: Proverbs 16:9
Objective: To learn to rely on God for guidance
Materials needed: Stargazing app for your phone
(Sky Map for Android or Star Walk for iPhone),
blankets, telescope (optional)

Date #8:
Dress for Success

Challenge activity: A Celebration Date
with Mom and Dad
Key verses: Ephesians 5:31-32
Objective: To begin to view marriage as a picture of
God's love for his people.
Materials needed: A reservation at a restaurant,
a few index cards, a pencil or pen—and most important,
your daughter's mom!

Step 4: Talk with Dad

After you've experienced something through the Dad–Daughter Challenge, you'll have a heart-to-heart with your girl to figure out what you can learn together. All the simple conversations, questions, and Bible verses you need are right there within the date for you—so you can guide your daughter in a growing understanding of boys and what it means to be a girl. To make this more fun for her, we offer "Talk with Dad" pullout pages in the back of this book. She can doodle, fill in the blanks, and even tape mementos and photos of your date to these pages. (In case that sounds perfectly horrible to you, Dannah assures me that those are things many girls like doing!)

Each date's "Talk with Dad" gives you the complete text of your daughter's pullout pages, including all the clues, answers, and other stuff that your daughter will fill in. So don't be surprised when your "Talk with Dad" suddenly begins talking to your daughter!

Step 5: Finish Strong

A simple prayer about what you've just learned is a great way to end the date.

**Okay, let's get started with Date #1.
It's time to pull a few pranks!**

PART 2

8 Great Dates

Challenge activity: Adventure Pranking 101

Key verse: Jeremiah 29:11

Objective: To begin to understand boys as a part of God's good plan

Materials needed: Supplies for your favorite practical joke, or one of mine

Step 1: Prep Talk

Lexi was four years old and we had a problem: she loved being as naked as a jaybird and streaking through our house.

One day, her older brother, Robby, had some friends over. They were playing ball in the backyard when The Streak made her public debut by running through first base. Dannah had some kind of important talk with her. It must have shocked Lexi into a whole new reality. That night when she went to change into her pj's, she slammed the door and shouted, "Dad, you can't see me. Boys and girls are different."

And so began the life lessons in understanding boys. And girls. And how they're different.

I'll confess that raising a daughter can be about as perplexing as figuring out how astronauts go to the bathroom...and about as awkward too! Imagine what it's like for her to try to understand boys, especially if she doesn't have a brother.

One very simple truth that can anchor everything we try to understand in life is this:

"'I know the plans I have for you,' declares the Lord, *'plans to prosper you and not to harm you, plans to give you hope and a future'" (Jeremiah 29:11).*

God has a plan for your life. He has a plan for your daughter's life. And he had a plan from the beginning of creation—including the distinct creations of Adam and Eve—for something called marriage. In an age of gender dialogue that'll make the most mature head spin, perhaps an important underpinning conversation is simply the truth that God had a plan!

Anchoring your discussion about gender into God's perfect plan will enable her to continually look to God's Word for his truth about boys and girls, men and women, marriage and motherhood.

THE 4 RULES OF PRANKING

1 The prank *should be relatively easy to clean up.* There's a fine line between a prank and vandalism. When I was a kid, I saw a car in my neighborhood that was covered in syrup and straw. (A twist on tarring and feathering.) That's not okay. Do not tar and feather anyone. (Although there is an interesting tar-and-feather scene in HBO's epic *John Adams* miniseries—which is awesome—but let's get back to the point.)

2 In the end, the prank *should be as much fun (almost) for the victim* as the pranksters.

3 The prank *must not risk any real damage* to items.

4 The prank *must be creative* (not the same old short-sheeted bed that your grandpa did).

PLANNING DATE #1
Mission Possible!

All right, it's time to have some fun. When we started writing this date, we went looking for good pranks in the Bible. While we didn't find any biblical evidence of short-sheeted sleeping mats or camels with a banana in their...well...anyway...we did talk about Laban tricking Jacob into marrying the wrong daughter (Leah) after seven long years of labor. (Note—that was a real loser move.) The problem with this prank is that it breaks the first two of our rules of pranking. It's not easily cleaned up, and it wasn't fun for the victim, Jacob, who had to work another seven years in order to marry the woman he loved (Rachel)! Okay, that's about as close of a connection as we are going to make to pranks and the Bible. Now let's get on with the mission!

1. Read through the rest of the date.

2. Choose a prank and collect the materials you need to pull it off. (You may want to let your daughter help you choose the prank.)

BOB'S FAVORITE PRACTICAL JOKES

Each of the jokes revealed to you here today has been successfully executed, and the targets of the pranks lived to laugh about it. *("$ to $$$" indicates how much cash you'd need to put out for this idea.)*

The tried-and-true ding-dong-ditch. If you need to start off real slow, try the old ring-the-doorbell-and-run trick. I know it's old and just about worn out, but it's probably new for your girl. Leave some cookies on the doorstep for a neighborly touch.

The fishbowl $. I did this to Dr. Pat Sullivan, the principal of the high school we founded. Buy dozens of goldfish. *Dozens!* (They are cheap.) Sneak into someone's apartment or house when they are gone and fill each and every container you can with a few scaly friends. The toilets. Water cooler. Sinks. Glasses. Cups. Bowls. Leave no cavity un-finned. On a smaller scale, you could do this in *one* family bathroom to prank just one or two individuals. In that case fill the bathtub too!

The Annoy-a-tron $. Spend $12.95 and purchase an Annoy-a-tron. This gadget is the size of a thick quarter but will drive your target crazy! You'll hide it somewhere in his or her office, bedroom, or house. It chirps, whispers "Can you hear me?" and makes other annoying sounds at random intervals so it's impossible to figure out where the sound is coming from. Jarrod put this device in the ceiling in my office one time, and it took me about an hour of madness to find it. It all worked out, though. I got him back by unscrewing the telephone outlet in his wall and putting the device in there. (It took him weeks to find it.)

Foiled again! $$$. Buy a trunk load of extra-wide aluminum foil and head over to your target's property. Identify a car or truck. *Carefully* cover each and every square inch of the vehicle with foil until it looks like something ready to fly into outer space.

Surprise shower. Wrap a rubber band around the kitchen sink sprayer so whoever turns on the faucet gets a big, wet surprise.

Who turned off the power? This one is simple but fun. All you need to do is slightly unscrew all of the lightbulbs in your victim's home. Don't take them out all the way; just turn them enough that they don't make contact. Your victim will think they have burned out. (If you know where they are, you should hide all of their spare lightbulbs!)

Extreme home makeover. Okay—this one takes some planning and requires just the right friends to be accomplices. And they'll have to be well off and have a really big house…and you'll have to ask to borrow it for a night. Stage the home to look like it is yours. Replace all the family photos. Bring your beloved dog over…and his toys. Then, invite some friends over who have never been to your house before. Let them marvel at your newfound fortune. (When I helped mastermind this one, it was with out-of-town guests. We even let them put *their* pj's on and crawl into bed for the night before the big revelation!)

The key to this one is to let your house guests become more and more incredulous as the hours pass by. The reveal has to be done in such a way that makes everyone laugh. You might invite the real home owners in to ask if they can have their house back, or "mistakenly" leave a monogrammed pitcher or family photo from the real owners in a strategic place. However your victims find out, this one is sure to be the stuff of legends for years to come. And it's *free*!

🔧 PREP FOR LIFE

- ■ If you purchase something online for your prank you can teach your daughter how to do this safely. Let her enter the shipping and billing information. (This is also a good reinforcement for learning your address and phone number.)

- ■ If you go with the lightbulb prank, you can teach your daughter how to safely change a lightbulb. (Don't forget: *lefty-loosie, righty-tightie*.)

- ■ Don't like our prank ideas? Go searching for your own on the Internet. Again, you can teach her online safety.

Step 2: SKG Radio for Your Ride to the Challenge

Play *Date #1: Mission Possible!* either en route to your victim's home or in a super-secret place in your house if your victims live in the same house you do.

Step 3: Dad-Daughter Challenge

Execute your prank together. As you do, emphasize the fact that it is *possible* for your daughter to execute the mission. Encourage her that she can do anything she puts her mind to.

MOVIE ENCORE!

A great follow-up movie for this date is *Big Fat Liar* (not to be confused with *Liar, Liar!*). Although it may be the ultimate children's practical-joke movie, it also carries a great emphasis on integrity and truth.

Step 4: Talk with Dad

After your prank, find a fun place to talk. Maybe go out for ice cream on the way home or just pull a gallon out of the freezer and teach her to eat guy-style, straight from the carton.

Pull out "Date #1: Mission Possible!" from our Talk with Dad Pullouts in the back of this book. Give them to your daughter and talk through them, giving her time to fill in the blanks.

Talk with Dad
Mission Possible! Understanding Boys

Remember, the following section is a copy of what we created for your daughter. It was written by Dannah and Suzanna for your girl. Turn to page 143 for the pullout version your daughter will use for this date.

Welcome to Secret Keeper Girl's 8 Great Dates for Dads and Daughters. You may have just committed your first practical joke! Congratulations. You took on the mission and successfully completed it. Another *possible* mission in life will be understanding boys!

Read Jeremiah 29:11 and fill in the blanks:*

> "'I know the ___*plans*___ I have for you,' declares the LORD,
> '___*plans*___ to prosper you and not to harm you,
> ___*plans*___ to give you hope and a future.'"
>
> Jeremiah 29:11

Based on that verse, fill in this blank:

> God has a ___*plan*___ for my life.

He must also have a plan for the fact that boys are in your life. While that may not include marriage, it most likely will. God's plan for a girl in the Bible named Rebekah included marriage. She was a few years older than you when this story took place.

---

* The "Talk with Dad" sections give you all the clues, answers, and so on that your daughter will write in the blanks in her pullouts. So don't give away too much!

Rebekah was just an ordinary, everyday girl who was respectful of her parents. One day, while going about her daily task of getting water for her family, she met a visitor from a distant land who was in need of water for himself and his camels. Interested in the opportunity to meet someone from a land that she had only heard of, she offered to draw water from the well for the man and his animals. She could not have known that this simple act of service would change her life. The traveler she helped was actually Abraham's servant, who had been sent on an adventure of his own. He had been sent to locate a wife for the son of his master, Abraham, in the land of their origin. The servant's name was Eliezer, and he prayed to God for help in completing the mission Abraham had assigned to him. This is what he asked of God:

> *"See, I am standing here beside this spring, and the young women of the town are coming out to draw water. This is my request. I will ask one of them, 'Please give me a drink from your jug.' If she says, 'Yes, have a drink, and I will water your camels, too!'—let her be the one you have selected as Isaac's wife. This is how I will know that you have shown unfailing love to my master."*
> Genesis 24:13-14 NLT

Does his request sound familiar? Yes, because that's exactly what Rebekah did! By embracing and seeking out God's adventure for her life in her everyday activities, she was led to marry Abraham's son. She would become the grandmother of 12 young men. These young men would grow up to be the leaders of the 12 tribes that form the nation of Israel. And Rebekah? She would be the great, great, great, great, great, great, great (insert 30 more "greats")...grandmother of Jesus. And the beginning of this great adventure happened while she was doing her daily chores. (Think about that the next time your mom asks you to empty the dishwasher or take out the trash!)

—by Jarrod

God had a plan for Rebekah: to be one of the ancestors of Jesus!

And that plan included a boy named Isaac (who drove a really nice camel).

Not bad. Not bad at all.

Dad, explain that your daughter may or may not have the adventure of marriage in her future, but God does have a good plan either way. The important thing is to trust his plan—to trust him as she begins to discover and understand boys and discover and understand her own purpose as a girl.

Talk with Dad about the following questions and write your answers in the blanks as you discuss the *very possible* mission of understanding boys.

- Who do you think likes practical jokes better—boys or girls?

- What are some differences you've observed when you compare boys and girls?

- Why do you think God created boys and girls to be so different?

- What plans do you think God *might* have for your life?

- You probably won't find a husband by giving water to camels, but do you hope you'll be married one day? Why or why not?

Step 5: Finish Strong

End today's date by praying with your daughter and asking God to fill her with a strong sense of certainty that he has a plan for her life. It may or may not include a boy, but it will be a great plan. Invite her to pray too.

Sugar and Spice and Everything Nice

Challenge activity: Recipe for Success

Key verses: Proverbs chapter 31

Objective: To begin to understand what it means to be a girl

Materials needed: Baking ingredients, an empty kitchen

Step 1: Prep Talk by Jarrod

A great tradition I have with my daughter is that we cook breakfast together for our family almost every Sunday morning. At first we tried making different things each week. But with the purchase of a $30 waffle maker we have settled into a ritual of making chocolate-chip waffles.

The morning begins when I wake her up by playing the song "Good Time" from my phone. She slides out of the top bunk onto my back and I piggyback her down the stairs and plop her onto the kitchen counter. We then begin assembling the ingredients with great stealth, because the recipe we have developed over the last three years is a carefully guarded secret. We cook  the waffles to just the right consistency and then bury them in chocolate chips, whipped cream, and our favorite syrup.

We have made hundreds of waffles over the last three years. But more than that, we have made memories that will last a lifetime. Today we want to challenge you to build a memory with your daughter by doing something that also enables you to talk about traditional stereotypes of girls and boys.

JUST FOR KICKS

My kids still talk about this meal I made eight or ten years ago. I'll bet your daughter will too. (It doesn't taste great, but it's fun.)

Bob's Dishwasher Salmon

4 (6-ounce) salmon fillets
4 tablespoons freshly squeezed lemon juice
1/2 teaspoon salt
1/2 teaspoon freshly ground black pepper
Heavy-duty aluminum foil

1 Cut 2 12-inch-square sheets of aluminum foil. Place 2 fillets side by side on each square and fold up the outer edges. Drizzle 1 tablespoon of lemon juice over each fillet. Season with salt and pepper. Fold and pinch the aluminum foil extra tightly to create a watertight seal around each pair of fillets. Make sure the packet is airtight by pressing down on it gently with your hand. If air escapes easily, rewrap. *Do not attempt to cook a whole fish.*

2 Place fish packets on the top rack of your dishwasher.

3 Add dirty dishes and lemon-scented soap. *This step is optional and is not recommended for novices.* However, as long as the salmon is tightly sealed in the aluminum foil, it will not absorb any soapy taste or smell.

4 Set the dishwasher to the "normal" cycle. Modern dishwashers have "economy" and "cool dry" settings, which are undesirable because they conserve heat. However, on the other end of the spectrum, the "pots and pans" setting tends to overcook the fish.

5 Run salmon through the entire wash-and-dry cycle: approximately 50 minutes for most models. (Don't have a dishwasher? Bake the foil-wrapped packets in a preheated 400° F. oven for 12 minutes.)

6 This dish is best served with a béarnaise sauce or something like that. You might want to buy a pre-made sauce or a seasoning packet you can combine with a couple of simple ingredients.

PLANNING DATE #2
Sugar and Spice and Everything Nice

Traditionally, women have the label of "family chef." As we were writing this book, Dannah and I discussed the real nature of biblical femininity and the stereotypes that go along with any discussion of it. The traditional Christian view is that women are gentle, nurturing, and kind. While we certainly agree with that, we also began to consider other aspects of the Proverbs 31 woman. That chapter states that she "sets about her work vigorously" and "her arms are strong for her tasks."

The qualities of a woman are diverse and complex. We do believe in biblical headship within marriage, but in no way does that subjugate the woman and put her in a role where she cannot do amazing things like owning a business or buying land (see Proverbs 31). Biblical femininity is gentle, nurturing, and kind while still being strong and courageous at the same time.

We have to be very careful what labels we put on our daughters. The history of the church is riddled with demeaning labels for the roles of women—labels that put our daughters in boxes that God does not. And the world is countering with labels of its own, which demand independence and self-sufficiency. These also are contrary to God's perfect plan. A great way to talk about femininity, stereotypes, and labels with your daughter is to start in the kitchen, where women traditionally rule. But we're going to mix it up a bit (pun intended) and ask you, Dad, to put on your chef's hat:

1. Read through the rest of the date.
2. Buy or collect your ingredients before your date.
3. Choose which baking challenge to accept: Kitchen Hacker, Sous Chef, or Gourmet Guru.

Kitchen Hacker: So maybe your cooking experience is limited to burning water. (It has been done!) Don't worry—try this simple recipe.

When I visited Dannah's parents for the first time, her mom made a cool dessert I'll never forget. In fact, Purple Flurp is in one of Dannah's fiction books for tween girls: *Danika's Totally Terrible Toss*. Flurp is not the most nutritious dessert, but it's sure fun and easy!

Purple Flurp

1 can blueberry pie filling

1 can crushed pineapple, drained

1 can sweetened condensed milk

Mix the ingredients together and chill them (maybe while you do your Talk with Dad.)

Add 1 tub of whipped topping before serving.

Sous Chef: A little more ambitious? Grab your favorite tub of chocolate-chip cookie dough from the store or the fridge. With your daughter, pre-heat the oven and scoop the dough onto a nonstick baking tray. Follow the cooking directions on the package and voilà!—dessert is served. For a little extra pizzazz try our Killer Cookie "recipe."

Killer Cookies (serves two)

1 tub or tube of chocolate-chip cookie dough

1 container of vanilla ice cream

Chocolate syrup

Whipped topping

Optional ingredients: bananas, nuts, chocolate chips, maraschino cherries

Bake one extra-large chocolate-chip cookie for two using a portion of the cookie dough and the instructions on the package. While the cookie is still warm, use a spatula to place it in a large serving bowl. Top the cookie with huge scoops of ice cream, chocolate syrup, and whipped topping. Add other toppings or alter the flavor of ice cream as desired. Grab two large serving spoons and have a father–daughter feast that may become a tradition. You can do Talk with Dad while you eat if you like.

Gourmet Guru: If you are comfortable in the kitchen and are constantly whipping up delectable concoctions, try cupcakes—use a regular cake mix from the store (her favorite, perhaps). Look on the back of the box for the extra ingredients. Most cake mixes require eggs, oil, and water. Choose a tub of icing and some colorful sprinkles. Make sure you have cupcake baking liners at home, or purchase them at the store. Have a daughter that loves to decorate? Cupcakes are the perfect opportunity to let her go all out with fun sprinkles, different colored icing, piping bags. Maybe take her to the store and let her pick out what she wants.

Another option is to take a tip from Jarrod and get up with your daughter on a Saturday or Sunday morning to make waffles for the whole family. These, too, can be made from a box and require you to add only a few ingredients. (Don't forget the maple syrup.)

⚒ PREP FOR LIFE

■ Take your daughter to the grocery store with you and let her help find the ingredients. (She may be better at it than you are.)

■ When you make your way to the checkout, give her the money and let her take care of paying.

■ Have her figure out the calories and nutrition of the meal.

For something more challenging, teach your daughter the skill of communicating to people in need.

■ Take your creation—cookies, cupcakes or cake— to someone in need. Maybe it'll be the shut-in older couple down the street or a family who just had a baby in your church. The key to this Prep for Life task is to let her learn to do the talking. Have her ring the doorbell and explain that she wants to give them some cookies that she made and she hopes it'll encourage them. (You'll have to help her think of what to ask and say before you arrive.)

Step 2: SKG Radio Before the Challenge

Play *Date #2: Sugar and Spice and Everything Nice* in your own kitchen just before you begin.

Step 3: Dad-Daughter Challenge

Complete your baking or dessert challenge.

MOVIE ENCORE!

One of my favorite cooking scenes in the movies comes in *Cheaper by the Dozen*—the "cleanup on aisle 12" scene. Hopefully things didn't get this ugly in your kitchen! But watching this movie would make a great follow-up activity for you and your daughter.

Step 4: Talk with Dad

While you eat your dessert or wait for your Purple Flurp to set, complete the Talk with Dad time.

Pull out "Date #2: Sugar and Spice and Everything Nice" from our Talk with Dad Pullouts in the back of this book. Give them to your daughter and talk through them, giving her time to fill in the blanks.

Talk with Dad

Sugar and Spice and Everything Nice: Understanding Girls

Remember, the following section is a copy of what we created for your daughter. It was written by Dannah and Suzanna for your girl. Turn to page 147 for the pullout version your daughter will use for this date.

What amazing dessert did you and your dad just make? Draw a picture of it in the box below.

Dessert with Dad

To better understand how God has created boys and what makes them different, you need to understand how God has crafted and wired you. What makes you unique? Did you know that just like the special recipe that you prepared with your dad, your heavenly Father has a special recipe just for you? It's a top-secret recipe he has only used once, and that was when he made you. There is only one you, and there will never ever be anyone just like you. In the recipe card below, list some of the "ingredients" God used to make you. Under "directions," write down a good thing you can do with each "ingredient."

Dad, put your daughter's name in the blank. Then, you can encourage her by giving her some ideas for her "ingredients," such as a sense of humor, blue eyes, crazy math skills, a love for baking, and so on. Anything that helps make up your girl counts! "Directions" means, what good thing can she do with that "ingredient"? Maybe cheer up her friends, help somebody with homework, and so on.

Secret Keeper Girl   Recipe For _____

INGREDIENTS	DIRECTIONS

God created you to be marvelously unique and special. He made you a girl, who will grow into a woman. Do you know how wonderful that is? One chapter of the Bible honors an especially good example of womanhood. She is known as the "Proverbs 31 woman." Not all women will be like her, because Proverbs 31 is not a chapter with commands for what a woman *must* be, but an example of what a really exceptional woman *can* be.

Look at the verses below. With your dad, read each section out loud and then write an "ingredient" like "strength" or "hard-working" that describes what you just read.

Verses 10-12

A wife of noble character who can find? She is worth far more than rubies. Her husband has full confidence in her and lacks nothing of value. She brings him good, not harm, all the days of her life.

Ingredient: _____

Verses 13-15

She selects wool and flax and works with eager hands. She is like the merchant ships, bringing her food from afar. She gets up while it is still night; she provides food for her family.

Ingredient: _____

Verses 16-17

She considers a field and buys it; out of her earnings she plants a vineyard. She sets about her work vigorously; her arms are strong for her tasks.

Ingredient: _____

Verse 20

She opens her arms to the poor and extends her hands to the needy.

Ingredient: _____

Verses 24-25

She makes linen garments and sells them, and supplies the merchants with sashes. She is clothed with strength and dignity; she can laugh at the days to come.

Ingredient: _____

Verses 26-29

She speaks with wisdom, and faithful instruction is on her tongue. She watches over the affairs of her household and does not eat the bread of idleness. Her children arise and call her blessed; her husband also, and he praises her: "Many women do noble things, but you surpass them all."

Ingredient: _____

Verse 30

Charm is deceptive, and beauty is fleeting; but a woman who fears the LORD is to be praised.

Ingredient: _____

Talk with Dad about the following questions and write your answers together.

■ When was the last time your mom picked up some wool and flax or made linen garments? What does your mom do instead that would be like that?

■ How could we rewrite some of these verses to describe a modern-day Proverbs 31 woman?

■ What can you do to look like a Proverbs 31 girl?

_____

■ In the space below, work with your dad to make a list of the ingredients you want to have as a godly girl:

_____   _____

_____   _____

_____   _____

_____   _____

Step 5: Finish Strong

End today's date by thanking God for the specific ingredients he's used to create your daughter. Whether she's a tomboy or a girl who loves pink, God has chosen for her to be just the way she is. Ask her to thank God out loud for the way he's created her.

As You Wish

Challenge activity: Movie Night

Key verses: 1 Corinthians 13:4-8

Objective: To discover the difference between true love and counterfeit love

Materials needed: *The Princess Bride* movie, movie-watching munchables

Step 1: Prep Talk by Dannah

I was driving our daughter Lexi home from a long trip. It was just her and me. It was during that season when Bob and I had decided to separate for the purpose of learning to love one another again. Our poor kids felt the tension.

In a bathroom at Sea World (where I'd stopped to assuage my overdeveloped sense of guilt that it was the worst summer ever for my little girl), five-year-old Lexi stood in the corner of the room staring intently into my eyes, and she made a declaration.

■ **"You have tiger eyes," she said. "I'm not going with you."**

She said it very matter-of-factly. For a moment I considered how I might wrestle this small child into the minivan, and then I realized she was just expressing what her heart felt in the best way she knew. I think children have the ability to see into our hearts in those difficult times—those times when we don't exemplify love and are full of fury.

I don't know about you, but Bob and I have not always been the best examples of love for Lexi and Autumn and Robby. I'm so thankful that we learned long ago to ask forgiveness for those times and to talk openly about how hard it is to love well.

"Interviews with young adults suggest they want their initial marriage to last, but are not particularly optimistic about that possibility," stated researcher George Barna. No bride or groom plans to break the vows they solemnly and sometimes tearfully express to each other on their wedding day. But a Barna study indicates that one-third of American adults who have been married at least once have been divorced.[22] Sadly, such numbers no longer shock us. In fact, you may even know the pain of divorce in your own family. We're so sorry. (But we're so glad you've discovered these 8 Great Dates that can bond you together.)

Even if you haven't known the sting of divorce, we would put money on the possibility that you've struggled in your marriage. ■ **Marriage can be difficult, and we're not always the best examples for our children. It's okay to admit that.** And to tell your children that you're aiming for true love even if sometimes you miss the mark.

True love is a choice to put someone else above yourself. Hollywood has become the master counterfeiter when it comes to love and will train your daughter to think that love is about attraction. Teaching your daughter to discern when she is being fed a counterfeit message is essential. Dad, there is a world out there that will seek to steal your little girl's heart. It's your job to protect her from the pirates that would rob her of her innocence. Pirates like the "Dread Pirate Roberts," villain in *The Princess Bride*, who was well known for taking no prisoners.

The Princess Bride may be the greatest philosophical teaching movie of the twentieth century. (Okay…that's ridiculous, but we really like it a lot.) Let's use the film to identify the difference between counterfeit and true love on this date.

PLANNING DATE #3
As You Wish

It's fun to go out to the movies, but sometimes it's just as nice to stay at home and watch in the comfort and security of your own abode. For this date we want you to watch *The Princess Bride* together. You've probably seen it once or twice (or a hundred times) but this is one movie you just can't see too many times.

Nudge/push/kick Mom (and everyone else) out of the house and get down to business. (If you are having a hard time convincing Mom to leave, take this book to her and point to the next line.)

Mom, seriously, you have to go.

> *Note*: We have had extensive conversations among our team about whether we could use the word "kick," as in "kick Mom out of the house." You're intelligent. You understand, right? We are not advising you to actually kick anyone.

1. Read through the rest of the date.

2. Rent, purchase, or stream a copy of *The Princess Bride*. (This may take a little recon.) *Note: this movie is rated PG.*

3. Snacks: popcorn, and those sugar-filled, carbonated, caffeinated beverages that Mom doesn't ordinarily allow your kids to have in the house. Below are a few ideas of just how to do popcorn to spice up your date.

Movie-theater popcorn $$. How good can a movie experience be without genuine movie-theater popcorn? We highly recommend swinging by your local theater for a large popcorn just before you are set to start your movie. (If you love movie-theater popcorn, Monday night football is another good excuse to do this.)

Homemade popcorn $-$$$. For the hard-core pop-corners out there, teach your daughter to make homemade theater-style popcorn. This can be as easy as putting some oil in the bottom of a pot and adding popping corn. (Be sure to keep it moving!) After you've popped it, drench it in freshly melted butter and a touch of salt. Or you can use this date as an excuse to convince your wife to finally let you purchase a fantastic Whirley Pop popcorn maker. (That's what we have in the Gresh home. Best. Popcorn. Ever!)

Counterfeit popcorn $. Don't like those ideas? Okay... you can cheat (sigh). 1) Go to the kitchen. 2) Grab the microwave popcorn. 3) Insert into microwave. 4) Hit popcorn button.

⚒ PREP FOR LIFE

Finding *The Princess Bride* may prove to be your first challenge. Involve your daughter in your search to find it. Several life skills can come into play here:

■ Teach her how to safely use the Internet or your smart-phone app to locate a rental copy near you, or a copy that can be streamed to your player.

Other opportunities to teach life skills:

■ Show her how to use an ATM in order to purchase snacks for your date.

■ If you are paying by check, explain how to properly fill out a check.

■ Using a credit card at the local grocery store? Go through the self-checkout line and let her scan the items. (Don't tell anyone, but my friend Jarrod lets his kids sign the electronic signature pad!)

⋐⫶ TURBO BOOST THIS DATE

Of course, there's just something fun about taking the TV (and couch) outside. Set up to watch *The Princess Bride* in your backyard. Grab a blanket and your popcorn, curl up on the couch with her, and enjoy the movie.

Step 2: SKG Radio Before the Challenge

Play *Date #3: As You Wish* on your way to pick up movie popcorn or in your living room right before you start the movie.

Step 3: Dad-Daughter Challenge

Find a comfy spot on the couch, pop in your DVD of (or start streaming) *The Princess Bride*, relax, and enjoy the movie. (Be sure to laugh at all of the rhyming lines—"Anybody want a peanut?")

Step 4: Talk with Dad

After the ending credits, open this book and grab a few more snacks before settling in for a daddy–daughter discussion time.

Pull out "Date #3: As You Wish" from our Talk with Dad Pull-outs in the back of this book. Give them to your daughter and talk through them, giving her time to fill in the blanks.

Talk with Dad

As You Wish: True Love vs. Counterfeit Love

Remember, the following section is a copy of what we created for your daughter. It was written by Dannah and Suzanna for your girl. Turn to page 151 for the pullout version your daughter will use for this date.

True love. It took Buttercup awhile to realize it, but when Westley was saying, "As you wish" what he meant was "I love you." (Seriously, I didn't catch on to this until about the tenth time I watched it…or until Dannah explained it to me…I can't remember which.) The narrator goes on to tell us that what was even more amazing was the day she realized she loved him back. True love was born.

The Bible describes true love in 1 Corinthians 13:

> "Love is patient, love is kind. It does not envy, it does not boast, it is not proud. It does not dishonor others, it is not self-seeking, it is not easily angered, it keeps no record of wrongs. Love does not delight in evil but rejoices with the truth. It always protects, always trusts, always hopes, always perseveres. Love never fails."

A friend of mine once suggested that I replace every reference to the word *love* in that passage with my name, as a test to see how good I was at true love. Let's try it. Insert your name in the blanks below. (And consider how true the sentence ends up being.)

True Love Test

_____ is patient,

_____ is kind.

_____ does not envy,

_____ does not boast,

_____ is not proud.

_____ does not dishonor others,

_____ is not self-seeking,

_____ is not easily angered,

_____ keeps no record of wrongs.

_____ does not delight in evil
            but rejoices with the truth.

_____ always protects, always trusts,
            always hopes, always perseveres.

_____ never fails.

How did you do? (Hopefully you did a little better than I did the first time I tried it!) You can use this same test with others when you think they may be trying to sell you a counterfeit. Let me be specific. As you get older, boys are going to start to notice how beautifully God has created you and they are going to start to compete for your attention.

Some boys will offer you false love.

These boys will be the opposite of 1 Corinthians 13. Over time you'll see that they are untruthful, selfish, impatient, unkind, boastful, proud, dishonoring of others, easily angered, and all that other stuff. Run from them.

Some boys will carry with them a heart for true love.

These boys will be able to fill their name in the blanks and the sentences will be true.

A boy who offers you true love might be a little like Westley. What was the sentence he always spoke to Buttercup?

"As *you*   *wish* ."

In this way, he was putting her ahead of his own desires. He was really saying, "I love you."

Talk with Dad about the following questions and write your answers in the blanks as you discuss what true love looks like.

■ How hard do you think it is to grow into expressing true love?

■ What kinds of things might a boy who is offering you fake love ask for?

■ Who do you know who is an example of true love?

■ How did you do in the 1 Corinthians True Love Test? What areas do you need to work on improving?

Step 5: Finish Strong

End today's date by confessing to God where you have not shown true love. Let your daughter learn from you and follow your example by doing the same. Ask God to show you both how to grow in selfless love.

Sticks and Stones
(or the "Italian Job")

DATE #
4

Challenge activity: A Wilderness Adventure
Hike

Key verses: Psalm 62:5-6

Objective: To learn to believe that her value
comes from God, not a boy

Materials needed: Hiking shoes, water bottle,
snacks, and a bag to collect several rocks

Step 1: Prep Talk by Dannah

I was just heartbroken when I realized what was going on.
Certainly this wasn't happening.

Not yet.

But I could see it with my own eyes.

Physically, I saw a lanky little nine-year-old girl pulling her
body up onto the bathroom counter so she could lean into the
mirror. Her eyes scanned the reflection, studying...no, scruti-
nizing...until they sighted a victim—a slightly crooked tooth.
She began to press upon that little tooth with her tiny little fin-
gers. Her eyes became squinted, speaking loudly the criticism
she felt for this imperfection.

Spiritually, I saw a precious daughter of Christ entering for
the first time into a battle she'd face again and again and again.

I wanted to run into that bathroom and set the physical
world in order—to tell her we'd fix the tooth and to call the

65

orthodontist for an appointment that very day. Instead, I stood outside that bathroom door and called upon the heavenly hosts to set the spiritual world in order in one little girl's heart.

This date is about protecting something of tremendous value—your daughter's self-worth. Bob has titled it the "Italian Job." I'll let him explain.

From Bob: I'm referring to a job completed 500 years ago when the Italian artist Michelangelo was commissioned to create what became the Renaissance masterpiece *David.* It's a brilliantly executed marble sculpture that stands just over 17 feet tall. (I don't recommend doing an Internet search with your daughter for a picture of this sculpture. As you can tell from the photo, this particular rendering of David won't pass any of Dannah's modesty tests!)

Michelangelo was given a flawed piece of marble that another artist had started to work on but left in bad condition. It was literally a piece of rock that had been tossed aside. Some

 people wondered whether it was unusable. But the artist saw a priceless work of art in that hunk of rock.

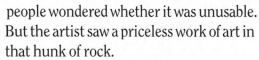 It's said that, one day while Michelangelo was in the process of sculpting *David*, the pope stopped by to check on his progress. Though it's not well documented, the pope allegedly marveled at the partially completed work and asked the great artist, "How do you know what to cut away?" Michelangelo replied, "It's simple—I just cut away everything that doesn't look like David."

God is in the sculpting business too. He is masterfully shaping each and every one of us, cutting away everything that doesn't

look like us. Your daughter's value comes from God. She needs to know that. She also needs to know that she can find her self-worth in the person he has shaped her to be, just like *David* finds its worth because of who shaped it. She needs to be able to find her self-worth in her relationship with God—not in boys, not in her friends, and not in her stuff. Ephesians 2:10 says,

> "We are God's masterpiece. He has created us anew in Christ Jesus, so we can do the good things he planned for us long ago" (NLT).

Your daughter needs you to help her see what a masterpiece the Master Sculptor is shaping her to be.

Research has shown a child's image of God correlates to that of her or his father. [23] Scary! Like it or not, you are the first representation of God that your daughter perceives (minus the big gut and receding hairline). You can guide your daughter to naturally believe in the goodness of God just by being a good dad.

 **SQUIRREL!**

Michelangelo's *David* is left-handed. So was Michelangelo. And Alexander the Great. So are Yogi Berra and Tim Tebow—and Bob!

PLANNING DATE #4
Sticks and Stones (or the "Italian Job")

This challenge will allow you to spend some quality time with your daughter out in nature. Be sure to bring along snacks and water; those short legs tire quickly.

1. Read through the rest of the date.

2. Plan where you will go on your wilderness adventure hike. Choose a trail that fits your style. Maybe making your way from the kitchen to the couch is your idea of a hike. Or maybe you summited Mt. Kilimanjaro last year. Either way, design your hike to suit your daughter's ability, not yours.

3. Consider the location of your adventure and get any items you need, such as hiking boots, water bottles, and snacks. Don't forget this book and a pencil and a small bag (see below).

⚡ TURBO BOOST THIS DATE

Go geocaching. Geocaching is a real-world, outdoor treasure-hunting game using GPS-enabled devices. Participants navigate to a specific set of GPS coordinates and then attempt to find the geocache (container) hidden at that location. Check out geocaching sites on the web for more information. I'm sure there's an app for that!

While you are on your hike you will help your daughter look for and collect seven rocks. Be sure to find small ones—don't be a hero. You'll use these for an object lesson that we've provided a script for. It's found at the end of this chapter in your version of the Talk with Dad section.

You'll need to locate

- ■ a smooth rock
- ■ a round rock
- ■ a colored rock (something different than the usual color of rocks in your area)
- ■ a rock that is broken

- a tiny pebble
- a rock the size of your fist (or a rock that's bigger than the others in your collection)
- a rock that is a unique shape

 **PREP FOR LIFE**

Following directions to arrive at a destination is a skill your daughter will need to use often in her life. Of course, nowadays there are many ways to successfully get from here to there.

- Teach her to use both a GPS and a map in this life-skills activity.
- Go online and have her look up the directions to your hiking destination. Teach her to use the GPS in your car to plot the course. If it fails to recognize a gravel road in the middle of nowhere, so much the better. This will show her she can't always rely on GPS (a mistake often made…not that I would know).

To navigate the hike:

- Give her a map and help her to follow it.
- Teach her how to use a compass. (If you need to, watch a YouTube video or consult another source first so you teach her correctly.)
- Help her to figure out how far you will be hiking by looking at the map scale.
- As you are on your way look for the trail markers; teach her what poison ivy looks like; identify trees or birds; look for wildlife; even make a game of who can spot the next creature first.

SQUIRREL!

Attention, overbearing-remote-controlling dads: Resist the temptation to just show your daughter. Allow her to actually do these things!

Step 2: SKG Radio for Your Ride to the Challenge

Play *Date #4: Sticks and Stones (or the "Italian Job")* in the car on the way to your hiking destination.

Step 3: Dad-Daughter Challenge

Embark on your wilderness adventure hike together. Enjoy nature and take any opportunity in your conversation to tell your daughter how much God values her.

MOVIE ENCORE!

Are you looking for an exciting *hiking* movie? Is there a more adventurous hike than the one Lucy takes through the wardrobe in *The Chronicles of Narnia: The Lion, the Witch and the Wardrobe*?

Step 4: Talk with Dad

After you have finished collecting stones or at the end of your hike, find a spot to sit down together. Read through your object lesson script and think about how to make our outline relevant to you and your daughter.

Pull out "Date #4: Sticks and Stones (or the 'Italian Job')" from our Talk with Dad Pullouts in the back of this book. Give them to your daughter and talk through them, giving her time to fill in the blanks.

Talk with Dad

Sticks and Stones (or the "Italian Job"): God's Masterpiece

Dad, we have provided you with a script for your object lesson to get you started. Feel free to elaborate—this is your chance to share. Turn to page 155 for the pullout version your daughter will use for this date.

Dad: Let's find somewhere to sit where we can look at our rocks. I want to talk about each one with you. Can you find the biggest one (the rock the size of your fist)?

Daughter: (Holds up the biggest rock.)

Dad: Now, of course we couldn't bring the biggest boulder we saw on our hike today with us. But just imagine that we could. If you were to stand on an island in the middle of a storm, would you rather be standing on that giant rock or some sand?

Daughter: A rock!

Dad: Well, did you know that God is called the rock many times in the Bible? Here, read Psalm 62:5-6.

Daughter: "Yes, my soul, find rest in God;
my hope comes from Him.
Truly He is my rock and my salvation;
he is my fortress, I will not be shaken."

Dad: In your life you will come into contact with people who will tell you that you are only good enough if you have the right stuff, hang out with the right people, or go to the right places. Those are lies that are like shifting sand. God is your rock and what he says to you is the truth. You can stand on the truth that you are God's child and that he created you to

be exactly the way you are. You don't need *anything* to make you "good enough." In God's eyes you are perfectly you.

Can you find the smoothest rock?

Daughter: (Holds it up.)

Dad: Jesus is like this rock. He is called the cornerstone. The cornerstone of a building is the most important stone. If it were removed the building would shake and fall. Jesus came so that we could be close to God—without him our sin would get in the way. Because of Jesus we can all be sons and daughters of God!

Can you find the round rock?

Daughter: (Holds it up.)

Dad: Do you know how many stones David used to take down Goliath?

Daughter: (The answer is one, but she might say five.)

Dad: Why do you think David had the courage to challenge Goliath?

Daughter: I don't know…because he knew God was on their side?

Dad: That's right. God was on David's side. Even though David was just a teenager, he knew that God was with him and God plus David was greater than Goliath. Just like God was with David, so he is with you. You don't have to ever be afraid of giants in your life. Sometimes giants could be unkind words that are spoken to you, disrespectful words spoken toward God, or sinful thoughts and ideas. God promises to always be near you no matter what is happening around you.

Can you find the broken rock?

Daughter: (Holds it up.)

Dad: God, our Father, cares about the times when we feel broken and sad. One time in my life that I felt sad was

_____

_____

God was there for me by _____

_____

This rock is to remind you that God will help you when you feel sad or broken. You can always go to him with all of your troubles.

Can you find the smallest rock?

Daughter: (Holds up the pebble.)

Dad: This rock is a reminder that God sees and cares about every little thing. You can talk to him about anything! One time when God answered my prayer was

_____

_____

Can you find the colored rock?

Daughter: (Holds it up.)

Dad: How is this rock different from the others?

Daughter: It is the color _____.

Dad: Yes, and like this rock, your relationship with God will bring joy and color into your life! He will give you ideas you couldn't think up yourself, he will give you love for people that you couldn't have by yourself—he will even lead you on some adventures you wouldn't have gone on without him!

Can you find the rock with the unusual shape—the unique rock?

Daughter: (Holds it up.)

Dad: What do you think it looks like?

Daughter: (Imaginative answer.)

Dad: This rock is to remind you of *you*. God created you to be unique—one of a kind. He knew you before you were born and loved you! And he wants to be close to you, so close that he is your Dad. First John 3:1 says, "See what kind of love the Father has given to us, that we should be called children of God." Always remember that your relationship with God is the most important one of your life. More important than your relationship with your friends. More important than boys. Even more important than your relationship with me, your mom, or your brothers and sisters. Always remember that you are his daughter—and that he loves you, created you, and is continuing to form you into what he planned you to become.

Step 5: Finish Strong

After the discussion, pray a simple prayer over your daughter. Pray that she would always know that God is her Father and find her identity in him as his daughter. Have her arrange her stones on her windowsill or dresser as a reminder of a great day with her Dad.

Challenge activity: A Treasure Hunt

Key verse: Proverbs 31:10

Objective: To discover that she is a treasure and should expect to be treated as one

Materials needed: Clues for the hunt, and a treasure—a piece of jewelry (can be simple and inexpensive, but make it special)

Step 1: Prep Talk

On Lexi's fifth birthday, I began thinking about how she'd leave me one day. And that some other guy would take my place. (It may have been premature. But am I the only melodramatic dad out there? Or have you thought about that too?)

Well, I didn't want to regret not making her feel special. I went out that day and bought her a simple gemstone bracelet. The gemstones were blue.

I bought a pewter box and had it engraved. It reads, "To Lexi from Daddy. December 28, 1998. Something blue." It's from the old wedding saying, "Something old, something new, something borrowed, and something blue." I just wanted to show her how much I valued her.

When we adopted Autumn at the age of 14, I began to include her in this special tradition. For the girls' sixteenth birthdays we found some old antique "tatting" (some kind of girly, lacey stuff) that was made by a great-aunt on Dannah's side of the

family. I commissioned embroidered handkerchiefs with the girls' names in them—"something old" to carry on their wedding day. (Okay, Dannah and her mom helped me a lot with this one.) I do hope my girls treasure these gifts—but more than that, I hope they feel treasured.

Let's build up your daughter's sense of value with a treasure hunt.

PLANNING DATE #5
Natural Treasure

Diamonds. They're just fancy rocks. And yet you may have spent weeks or months (or even years) of your pre-proposal days slaving away—flipping burgers on the side or selling ShamWow chamois (or attempting to sell a kidney on eBay)—trying to scrape together every penny you could in order to woo the love of your life into saying "yes" when you presented her with a little clear stone. Have you ever wondered what else is out there in the way of diamonds?

MOVIE ENCORE!

Well, as you might guess from the title of this date, we love the Disney film *National Treasure*, which is the ultimate treasure hunt. If you are looking for a follow-up film for this date you should check it out (even if it's for the twentieth time, if you're like us!).

The Cullinan diamond is the largest gem-quality diamond ever found. Uncut, it weighed in at 3106.75 carats. (That's 1.37 pounds!) The largest polished gem from that stone is named

Cullinan I or the Great Star of Africa, and at 530.4 carats it is the second-largest cut stone in the world. (That makes it a quarter-pounder.) From his knee, Prince William offered an 18-carat sapphire diamond formerly worn by his mother, Princess Diana, when he proposed to Kate Middleton. Then there's me, paying $1500 in 1988 to buy Dannah a .67 carat diamond, bought with the blood, sweat, and tears of years of ShamWow chamois sales.

■ **(Yes, I made a lot of money in college selling synthetic chamois at flea markets—way before that dude renamed them "ShamWows.")**

1. Read through the rest of the date.

2. Select your treasure-hunt location—a mall or downtown will do just fine.

3. Bring along $1 to $5 to complete a couple of the clues.

4. Cut out or photocopy the treasure-hunt clues. Or if you are a rhyming genius, create your own.

This challenge will take you on a race around the mall or around town. We have provided you with some clues (feel free to create your own) for this treasure hunt. So all you will need to do is photocopy them and hand her the first one.

You will need a "treasure" to give to her (or hide for her) at the end of the hunt. It could be a sterling-silver necklace with a heart, a charm bracelet with a few meaningful charms attached, or a pair of earrings with her birthstone. It doesn't have to be expensive or flashy—just something unique that will last.

SQUIRREL!

While I was writing this, I went on eBay and bought a rock…from China. I searched for uncut stones and bought a 155-gram amethyst crystal specimen for $10 (plus $6 shipping.) You might want to try this. It's fairly cheap…and your girl will love it.

After giving her the first clue, you will give your daughter each clue when she finds or spots the item in the previous one. We have given you 15 clues, so use your discretion. Don't use all of them if she is getting tired of the hunt or you are having difficulty finding a few of the things. You will give the first clue to her at home. Give her hints that direct her toward the mall (or downtown) after she reads the second. The final clue points to your jacket pocket, but if you are able to hide the treasure somewhere clever, create your own final clue to lead her to it.

Treasure Hunt Clues

1. We might go near or we might go far,
   Find your next clue in the car.

2. Let's go, go, go—we've just begun
   Find lots of shoppers on the run.

3. Look high and look low to get your next clue
   Find a shirt on which is the number "2."

4. Let's keep on going, just as planned
   Spot a couple holding hands.

5. Whether a reptile, insect, or mammal
   You must find your favorite animal.

6. Did you happen to skip your lunch?
   Buy a soft pretzel and munch, munch, munch!

7. Use your eyes and take a look
   Find the word "love" in a book.

8. Close your eyes, follow your nose
   Find a nice smell, tell your dad what you chose.

9. Let's keep going, faster and faster
   Find a sign and read it backward.

10. You're doing just great, just don't quit!
    Find a 99-cent item and buy it.

11. Laughter is the best medicine, so they say
    Spot someone laughing, ha, he, ho, hey!

12. Who could be the belle of the ball?
    Try on a fancy dress and do a twirl!

13. Stand quite still and use your ears
    Tell your dad how many different sounds you hear.

14. It might be tricky to get your last clue
    For first you must spot a bright-pink shoe.

15. Maybe the treasure's been here all the while
    Look in your dad's pocket—it might make you smile.

 TURBO BOOST THIS DATE

Okay, this one takes a little planning but is a lot of fun and comes highly recommended. No. Not just highly recommended. Listen to me like you've never listened before. (I'm not talking about "acting" like you're listening, like we all do with our wives at the end of a close football game. I'm talking about "straining-till-your-eardrums-hurt" kind of listening.)

Instead of hiding the gift you have for her in your pocket, have it waiting at the final stop of your scavenger hunt. Let's say your final stop is the ice-cream stand in the mall. You could work it out with the store manager ahead of time to present your daughter with the gift you have selected for her ahead of time.

This is pure gold.

You could also have a waitress bring it out with dessert or have it waiting at a drive-through window somewhere. The possibilities are endless. (Obviously you will need to rewrite the last clue to do this.)

Step 2: SKG Radio for Your Ride to the Challenge

Play *Date #5: Natural Treasure* in the car when you drive to your treasure hunt.

Step 3: Dad-Daughter Challenge

Complete your treasure hunt. Be sure to tell your daughter how much you love her when you give her the "treasure" and explain its meaning.

⚙ PREP FOR LIFE

■ Pay it forward. While you are in the mall, try one of my favorites, *Pay It Forward*. This one is easy and always worth every penny spent. All you need to do is a simple, random act of kindness for someone you don't know. This can be as simple as paying for the person behind you in the pretzel line, buying flowers for an elderly lady, or washing someone's windshield while they pump gas. (Be careful with that one. Ask permission first.) Another idea a friend of mine had was to bake cookies for the local police or fire department. (Avoid the temptation to go with donuts on this one.) You can never go wrong with teaching your daughter tangible ways to show love and appreciation to others.

■ Did you enjoy your treasure hunt? Another idea is to help your daughter create a treasure hunt for someone else in your home. They will have a great time doing it, and she could even "teach" them the lesson you shared with her following your treasure hunt. (I guess this is just another way to pay it forward!)

Step 4: Talk with Dad

Find a spot on a bench somewhere to have your discussion. Sometimes big crowds of people can bring anonymity. Or sometimes they can just be a distraction. Choose a place that suits you both.

Pull out "Date #5: Natural Treasure" from the Talk with Dad Pullouts in the back of this book. Give them to your daughter and talk through them, giving her time to fill in the blanks.

How can your daughter treat herself like a treasure? The Talk with Dad time will help you both discuss this question.

She'll probably be able to come up with ways to treat herself well on her own (and with your help), but here are five helpful hints if she gets stuck.

1. Body. Ways to take care of and respect her body include keeping herself clean and wearing modest clothing. Ways to disrespect her body include not properly taking care of herself (for example, not brushing her teeth and hair, not clipping her fingernails) and wearing immodest clothing.

2. Emotions. Positive ways to engage her emotions: exerting self-control, exhibiting emotion over normal situations in life, being passionate about people and things she cares about. Negative ways to engage her emotions: lack of control, exhibiting emotion (drama) over petty things (boys included—remember three-year-old Cody!).

3. Thoughts. Good, positive things to think about include what is listed in Philippians 4:8: thoughts that are true, honorable, just, and so on. Negative things to think about include worries, angry thoughts, and obsessive thoughts (about what her friends think of her or about boys).

4. Time. There are lots of options for good things to spend time on, some of which are unique to your daughter. Negative ways to spend time: wasting it and spending too much of it with media are biggies.

5. Energy. Good things to do: again, there are lots of options for this one—she shouldn't have any trouble here. Things that you shouldn't do: this will vary depending on the personality of your daughter. Maybe she wastes her energy pouting, or maybe she has a tendency to gossip or talk negatively about people or situations.

Talk with Dad

Natural Treasure: Learning My Value

Remember, the following section is a copy of what we created for your daughter. It was written by Dannah and Suzanna for your girl. Turn to page 161 for the pullout version your daughter will use for this date.

In 1980, a man named Kevin Hillier took his metal detector  out for a walk near the town of Kingower in Australia. Imagine his excitement when he found a gold nugget! And not just any gold nugget—**this shiny piece of metal weighs 61 pounds and is the largest known gold nugget in existence.** Its name is the Hand of Faith (in my opinion, it looks like a bullfrog if viewed sideways!).

Gold, silver, pearls, emeralds, diamonds, rubies. Such precious metals and gems have long been sought by treasure hunters. But do you know what is more valuable than all of the gold and diamonds found in the earth? You! In fact, God not only knows what color hair you have, he knows *how many hairs* you have on your head. [24] In his eyes, you are precious. In your dad's eyes, you are precious. One day your husband will think you are precious and will tell you he loves you more than anyone in the world.

Let's look at Proverbs 31:10 again. It says, "A wife of noble character who can find? She is worth far more than rubies."

What woman, if she had a beautiful diamond necklace, would wear it to dig in the garden or while she was going swimming? When something is precious we treat it well and take care of it.

How much more should you take care of *you*? Let's look at some ways that you can treat yourself like a treasure.

Talk with Dad about the following verses and questions and take some time to fill in the blanks.

1. Body

"Do you not know that your bodies are temples of the Holy Spirit, who is in you, whom you have received from God?" (1 Corinthians 6:19).

Treasure—what's a good way to take care of your body?

_____

_____

Trash—what's a way you can disrespect your body?

_____

_____

2. Emotions

"Above all else, guard your heart [inner part, mind, will, emotions], for everything you do flows from it" (Proverbs 4:23).

Treasure—what's a good way you can use your emotions?

_____

_____

Trash—what's a bad way you can use your emotions?

_____

_____

3. Thoughts

"Whatever is true, whatever is noble, whatever is right, whatever is pure, whatever is lovely, whatever is admirable—if anything is excellent or praiseworthy—think about such things" (Philippians 4:8).

Treasure—what are some good thoughts to dwell on?

_____

_____

Trash—what are some bad thoughts to dwell on?

_____

_____

4. Time

"Be very careful, then, how you live—not as unwise but as wise, making the most of every opportunity" (Ephesians 5:15).

Treasure—what's a good way to spend your time?

_____

_____

Trash—what's a bad way to spend your time?

_____

_____

5. Energy

"'Love the Lord your God with all your heart and with all your soul and with all your strength and with all your mind'; and 'Love your neighbor as yourself'" (Luke 10:27).

Treasure—what's a good thing to spend your energy on?

_____

_____

Trash—what's a bad thing to spend your energy on?

_____

_____

Step 5: Finish Strong

Use some of the things you learned about your daughter during your Talk with Dad to pray over her body, heart, mind, and so on. Give her the chance to pray too.

How Does Your Garden Grow?

Challenge activity: Plant Something

Key verses: Psalm 1:1-3

Objective: To grow by feeding herself with God's Word

Materials needed: Seeds or a plant, a place to plant it or them

Step 1: Prep Talk

We own a little ten-acre farm...and Dannah and I try to keep it looking really nice. This is not a good idea for recovering perfectionists. I try to keep the grass nice. All the while, there are various peacocks, chickens, goats, llamas, horses, and UPS delivery trucks occasionally wandering/galloping/skidding/grazing/driving/fertilizing, and generally destroying my nice green grass. (Okay. I will admit that last year while plowing through deep snow, I miscalculated and plowed up a significant piece of the tundra instead.)

Either way, each spring, it's time to patch the grass from all of these blunders. I'm fairly good at buying the seed and pretty good at spreading it around. But I am terrible at watering it. Meanwhile, my two fainting goats, Mayzie and Sour Kangaroo (don't ask), love to eat Dannah's prized flowers, which she does water and care for very well. All of this boils down to two pieces of advice (and one warning) when trying to grow anything, including a vibrant relationship with Christ:

1. Plant well.
2. Water well.
3. *Warning*: Don't let the goats get you down.

SQUIRREL!

Speaking of goats, did you know that coffee was allegedly discovered by an Ethiopian goatherd, a man named Kaldi? He observed that when his flock nibbled on the bright red berries of a certain bush they became more "energetic." As legend has it, Kaldi gave some of the berries to a disapproving holy man, who promptly tossed them into a fire. Then a tantalizing aroma arose. The roasted beans were sifted from the fire, ground up, and dissolved in hot water, yielding the world's first cup of coffee. What is it with holy men and caffeinated drinks? I mean, cappuccino was named after the brown-colored cowls that cover the shaven heads of the friars in the Capuchin order.

Just like grass, we all need to be watered. We all need to be fed. After 40 days of going without food, even Jesus got hungry. And do you know what his response was when Satan challenged him to go all Son-of-the-Creator-of-the-universe on a rock and make it become bread? He said, "No! The Scriptures say, 'People do not live by bread alone'" (Luke 4:4 NLT). The most important lesson you can teach your daughter is that she needs her own personal relationship with Jesus. Once she has that relationship, it's imperative that she grows in it. The best way to grow in her relationship with Jesus is to water it with the Word of God.

Psalm 1:1-3 says, "Blessed is the one who does not walk in step with the wicked or stand in the way that sinners take or sit in the company of mockers, but whose delight is in the law of the Lord, and who meditates on his law day and night. That person is like a tree planted by streams of water, which yields its fruit in season and whose leaf does not wither—whatever they do prospers." Who doesn't want their daughter to prosper? The best way for her to prosper is for her to learn to read God's Word on a regular basis. Now let's learn a little more about planting and watering and growing.

 # A TRULY WEEPING WILLOW
By Jarrod

A few years ago on Memorial Day we planted a weeping willow tree right in the middle of our front yard. We made a really big deal of it and talked about what a fun tree it would be to climb in the years to come. A few weeks later, I was proudly learning to use my new zero-turn mower (mowing now seemed more like playing Pac-Man than a household chore)—and I zero-turned right over our newly planted prize willow. I snapped it almost completely off about a foot and a half above the ground. Eighty percent of it was parallel to the ground. The kids and I promptly made a "splint" for the tree using duct tape and leftover tomato stakes. We have spent the last three years babying this little willow, and today it is alive and doing well! My kids will never forget the adventures with our Memorial Day willow.

PLANNING DATE #6
How Does Your Garden Grow? (by Suzanna)

1. Read through the rest of the date.

2. Collect the supplies you need for completing your mission. This may be a paperwhite narcissus for your daughter's windowsill (see below), or a perennial or outdoor shrub if the season is agreeable. We have several options for you.

A winter windowsill. The first option is to buy your daughter a paperwhite narcissus or other plant that you can force. Grown from bulbs, these flowers require no more than sunlight and water to produce fragrant blooms. This will be a great reminder to her of the lesson she learns with you about growing in God.

A second option is to grow indoor tulips. Fill a narrow glass container about a third of the way full with glass marbles or decorative rocks. (Clear glass will enable you to watch the roots develop.) Set the tulip bulb on top of the marbles or stones. Add water and some patience.

MOVIE ENCORE!

A couple of great growing movies (plants and people) are *The Secret Garden* (or read this aloud) and *Faith Like Potatoes*.

Perennial power. By planting a perennial flower—a day-lily, hosta, hydrangea, lily of the valley, or daisies, to name a few—with your daughter, you can create a memory that will last for years to come. It will give her something to look forward to in the coming springs as she waits in hope for the special flower she planted with you to bloom again and again. Before you start planting, examine your yard for some potential locations. Settle on one or two and then head out to your local greenhouse. Select a perennial that is appropriate for your climate. Involve your daughter in the selection process and ask her opinions on what she likes and why. (Girls love to share their opinions, and they love to know that you care to listen to them.) Take your new plant home and let her help you plant it. I would encourage you to let her do as much of the work as possible. (This is always a challenge for dads...but get out of her way.) Don't forget to add water!

A legacy planting. Planting a tree provides a memory that can last for a lifetime along with adding beauty to your home. If you have room in your yard, find a special spot and add a tree. Make a day of it by taking your daughter to your local nursery and letting her help select it. Involve her in selecting the location, digging the hole, and positioning it just right. Make a big deal of her opinions, and resist the dad-temptation to let her watch as you do all the work. Trees also add some responsibility and depth to this date, as it is important to continue watering newly planted trees every day. Those watering times serve as a good reminder that we need to be watering ourselves with God's Word daily. (Flowering shrubs are a great option as well!)

Step 2: SKG Radio for Your Ride to the Challenge

Play *Date #6: How Does Your Garden Grow?* when you drive out to pick up your bulb(s) or tree.

Step 3: Dad-Daughter Challenge

The planning is part of the fun for this date, so be sure to choose your plant, choose the perfect spot, and plant it *together*.

 PREP FOR LIFE

Spend a little time this week growing your relationship together. If you are a fix-it dad and spend Saturdays doing repairs, let your daughter help you. Teach her some simple skills that are appropriate for her age.

If your expertise lies in a different direction, take a little bit of time to let her be a part of some of the tasks you do on a weekly basis. Maybe you are a dad who loves to cook, so let her be your sous chef. Maybe you are a computer whiz, so teach her how a computer program works. Maybe you know a lot about cars, so wash and wax your car together.

It doesn't matter *what* it is you do, just so long as you share it together. You will grow closer in the process.

Step 4: Talk with Dad

Spread a blanket out in your front yard or camp out on your couch to have your discussion time. Remember to water your plant again after you talk!

Pull out "Date #6: How Does Your Garden Grow?" from the Talk with Dad Pullouts in the back of this book. Give them to your daughter and talk through them, giving her time to fill in the blanks.

Talk with Dad
How Does Your Garden Grow?:
The Power of God's Word

Remember, the following section is a copy of what we created for your daughter. It was written by Dannah and Suzanna for your girl. Turn to page 165 for the pullout version your daughter will use for this date.

What is a seed? How can a little acorn turn into a giant oak tree? Jesus told a story about some seeds once.

> *"What do you make of this? A farmer planted seed. As he scattered the seed, some of it fell on the road, and birds ate it. Some fell in the gravel; it sprouted quickly but didn't put down roots, so when the sun came up it withered just as quickly. Some fell in the weeds; as it came up, it was strangled by the weeds. Some fell on good earth, and produced a harvest beyond his wildest dreams."*
>
> *Matthew 13:3-8* MSG

In order for a seed to sprout, grow, and eventually bear fruit a lot of things need to happen. It has to survive being eaten (by birds, bunnies, squirrels, or even you). It has to have a place to grow (there is no place for roots to grow in gravel). It has to have space to grow (no weeds). Above all, it needs good soil and life giving water. But when it does grow it produces lots of delicious things to eat. Just think of how much of our food comes from those little seeds. Yum!

You might have guessed that Jesus wasn't just talking about seeds in his story. He goes on to explain that the seeds in the story are God's love, the gospel.

"When anyone hears news of the kingdom and doesn't take it in, it just remains on the surface, and so the Evil One comes along and plucks it right out of that person's heart. This is the seed the farmer scatters on the road.

The seed cast in the gravel—this is the person who hears and instantly responds with enthusiasm. But there is no soil of character, and so when the emotions wear off and some difficulty arrives, there is nothing to show for it.

The seed cast in the weeds is the person who hears the kingdom news, but weeds of worry and illusions about getting more and wanting everything under the sun strangle what was heard, and nothing comes of it.

The seed cast on good earth is the person who hears and takes in the News, and then produces a harvest beyond his wildest dreams."

Matthew 13:19-23 MSG

I don't know about you, but I want to be the person who lets the seed of God's love grow in my heart until it is as tall and strong as an apple tree. One of the best ways that will help us to grow is to read God's Word, the Bible.

Just for fun, let's try a quiz. If you don't know the answers, you and your dad can figure them out together.

Quick Bible Trivia Quiz

What is the longest book of the Bible?
(Psalms)

Which person lived to be the oldest in the Bible?
(Methuselah)

How many books of the Bible share the story of Jesus (the Gospels)?
(four)

What three angels are mentioned by name in the Bible?
(Gabriel, Michael, and Lucifer)

How many disciples did Jesus have?
(12)

How many books of the Bible are named after women?
(Two—Esther and Ruth)

What is the shortest verse in the Bible?
(John 11:35—"Jesus wept.")

What are some of the instruments used to praise God in the Psalms?
(harp, timbrel, trumpet, lute, cymbals, stringed instruments)

What are the fruit of the Spirit? Can you name them all?
(love, joy, peace, patience, kindness, goodness, faithfulness, gentleness, self-control)

What's your favorite verse in the Bible?
(_____)

Facts are fun, but remember this: as we read God's Word and spend time with him, his love will grow and produce fruit in us.

Talk with Dad about the following questions and how you can both grow in God's Word. Be sure to take the Father–Daughter Devo Challenge that follows.

■ How has God's Word helped you grow already? (Hint: fruit of the Spirit)

■ Why do you think that reading the Bible helps you grow?

■ How often do you open God's Word and read it? Find a verse and commit it to memory this week.

Father–Daughter Devo Challenge

All right. It's time to get ready for some great God time together over the next several weeks. At the back of this book are seven devotions for you to read together. Do one devo a week for seven weeks, or go through all seven in one week. Choose what works best for you. Be sure, however, to set a day and time ahead of time to help keep you on track. Then just grab this book and jump right in! Start by reading the devotion aloud to each other.

Take the devo challenge a bit further by encouraging your daughter to read a daily devotional book. We recommend Dannah's *One Year Mother–Daughter Devo*. (Maybe you can place this strategically on the coffee table for your wife to find. What a change of roles that would be!)

Step 5: Finish Strong

Read and then pray the Lord's Prayer together. And ask God that his Word would stick to both of your hearts and help you grow. Pray specifically for ways your daughter wants to grow in her walk with God.

Challenge activity: Stargazing

Key verse: Proverbs 16:9

Objective: To learn to rely on God for guidance

Materials needed: Stargazing app for your phone (Sky Map for Android or Star Walk for iPhone), blankets, telescope (optional)

Step 1: Prep Talk

Fast-forward a few years. She walks onto the front porch holding his hand. She is completely aglow. You are completely ablaze. You stare at his torn blue jeans, black leather jacket, and bleached hair, wanting to pull that ring out of his lip with a pair of vise grips and put it…well…let's just say somewhere else. Who is this psychotic punk that has brainwashed your daughter and stolen her heart away from you? With his peach fuzz mustache he looks like a weird, barely postpubescent cross between Justin Bieber and Boy George. Does just the thought of this cause your blood pressure to rise? Can you feel your forehead beginning to sweat? I hope so, because mine is sweating just writing this. How could you let this happen? Where did you go wrong?

First of all, let me say that just because someone's wardrobe doesn't match your khaki-pants-and-sweater-vest standards doesn't mean that they are the Antichrist. Listen, I am sure

that you have all kinds of ideas about the man she is going to marry. And I am sure they are all good ideas—but what you really need to have is *God's* idea of the man that he has created for her. If you haven't started thinking about this, and this is a rude awakening, now's the time. You need to be praying for him. Now. Today. Tomorrow. And every day for the rest of your life. For your daughter, aside from choosing to have a relationship with God, deciding whom she marries will be the most important decision of her life. How do you prepare her for it? You teach her to look to the One who holds her destiny in his hand for guidance.

Your mission in this date is to teach her where to look for guidance every day (and night) of her life.

PLANNING DATE #7
The Final Frontier

This mission is for the techie in you. If you've been looking for an excuse to purchase a cool-looking stargazing app, here it is. (We promise not to tell your wife that there are great free ones out there.) If you are an Android user we recommend trying Sky Map (free). iUsers should check out Star Walk ($) for their iDevices. There are also great apps like Sputnik (for the iPhone) that track the positions and flyover times and locations of the *International Space Station* and satellites that are visible to the naked eye.

Check out an astronomy calendar just in case there is an interesting celestial event, such as a meteor shower or eclipse, that is occurring around the time when you want to have the date. If you really want to impress your daughter, read up on moon phases and planet facts. See the "Space Facts" sidebar for a few to get you started.

SPACE FACTS

- The average distance of the moon from the Earth is 239,000 miles. In other words, you could fit about 30 Earths stacked up between us and the moon.

- As of 2013, Jupiter has 50 confirmed, named moons and 17 more that have yet to be confirmed, for a total of 67.

- Many of our modern constellations were identified and named by the Greeks, who believed that heroes and beasts received a spot in the heavens for great deeds (which is why so many constellations have unpronounceable names).

- For centuries, sailors used Polaris, the North Star, to guide their ships.

- A "falling star" is actually a meteoroid that leaves a streak of light when it burns up upon entering the Earth's atmosphere.

- Pluto used to be classified as a planet. Now it is just called a "dwarf planet."

Now that you have hopefully tapped into your inner astronomy geek, scout out a good location for stargazing. It is best to think about this ahead of time. A wide open place with few trees and lights (such as a field) is ideal. At the very least, try to avoid places where there are a lot of streetlights.

1. Read through the rest of the date.

2. Check an astronomy calendar for any interesting sky events that may be coming up, and plan your date accordingly.

MOVIE ENCORE!

WALL-E is a must see movie if you are looking for something to watch with your daughter once you go back inside.

Do you prefer a classic? I bet she hasn't seen *E.T.*!

3. Collect blankets or chairs, a flashlight and snacks. (Optional—if it's a cool night some hot chocolate will go a long way to make this comfy and memorable.)

4. Download the stargazing app for your phone. (Alternate plan: check out a book on the constellations from your local library and take it along. Make sure your flashlight is powerful enough to light up the pages well.)

TURBO BOOST THIS DATE

To add an extra boost to your date, start your time with your daughter by taking a trip to a planetarium. You both will enjoy an astronomer's tour of the heavens and maybe learn a little something before your own stargazing adventure.

Or visit a science lab or a friend with a high-powered telescope for a closer look at the moon, planets, and stars. Some interesting celestial phenomena, such as Saturn's rings, are not visible to the naked eye but are with a telescope.

For you Magellans out there, you can try a nighttime hike using only the stars as your navigational guide. (I highly recommend taking a GPS or signal-flare gun, or leaving a trail of bread crumbs to find your way back, though. It's in every dad's DNA to overestimate his navigational skills.)

Step 2: SKG Radio Before the Challenge

Play *Date #7: Star Track—The Final Frontier* before you head out to the backyard, or in your car on your way to the stargazing destination.

Step 3: Dad-Daughter Challenge

The key to success for this activity is choosing a clear night. Once you have that, you are golden! Try to let your daughter talk (it shouldn't be hard) on this date. Remind her of God's faithfulness to be the North Star in her life.

🔧 PREP FOR LIFE

Teaching your daughter to locate the North Star is quite a prep-for-life lesson in itself. You will have a hard time, however, locating Polaris during the day.

You can take this date a step further by teaching her to correctly use a compass. (If you need some help on that yourself there is plenty of instruction available online.)

Step 4: Talk with Dad

Turn on your flashlight and open this book to this section once you have settled down on your blanket or in your chairs. Power up your phone and open the stargazing app.

Pull out "Date #7: Star Track—The Final Frontier" from the Talk with Dad Pullouts in the back of this book. Give them to your daughter and talk through them, giving her time to fill in the blanks.

As we have mentioned before, most girls are extremely verbal. (That means that they like to talk. A lot.) So conversations and discussions with your daughter have a meaningful impact on her heart. Consider taking a moment as you go through the Talk with Dad pages to share with her an experience in which you were guided by God. Particularly in a direction you would never have chosen for yourself. If it was difficult to trust God in that situation, tell her so. Be sure to conclude by explaining why you think he led you that way. And why his plan turned out to be better than your plan. She may not remember this lesson, but she will remember and be guided by your experience and example.

Talk with Dad
Star Track—The Final Frontier:
Let God be the North Star

Remember, the following section is a copy of what we created for your daughter. It was written by Dannah and Suzanna for your girl. *Turn to page 169 for the pullout version your daughter will use for this date.*

> Lord, our Lord, how majestic is your name
> in all the earth!
> You have set your glory above the heavens.
>
> *Psalm 8:1*

Our God is an amazingly extravagant God. There are more stars than we are able to count—and yet in another verse God says that he counts all of the stars and knows them each by name. Isn't he incredible?

Looking into the night sky (don't use your phone yet) see if you can see any constellations. How about planets? The North

Star, Polaris, is often mistaken as the brightest one in the sky. It's not, though. It actually ranks fiftieth in brightness.

To find the North Star you simply need to locate the Big Dipper (which is part of the constellation Ursa Major). The two outer stars of the Big Dipper's bowl point directly to Polaris. Polaris is also the last star in the handle of the Little Dipper (part of Ursa Minor). See if the two of you can spot it without technological help at first.

While all of the other stars in the night sky seem to change locations over time, Polaris just sits there night after night in the same spot. Should you ever find yourself lost in the dark, the North Star can be your guide out of the woods.

Enjoy exploring other constellations and planets using your phone app for help. (Be goofy: try pointing your phone at the ground to see what the sky looks like on the other side of the world.) Now try coming up with your own constellations. Maybe there is a group of stars that look like the outline of your pet or your favorite cartoon character. After all, that's pretty much what the Greeks did!

As I am sure you know, the planets in our solar system (including Earth) follow a path—an orbit—that circles the sun. The Earth's path is perfectly situated to allow for life to exist upon our little blue planet. If we were any closer to the sun we would burn up; any further and we would all be icicles. Isn't it wonderful that God placed the Earth on such a perfect path?

You are on a perfect path too. And God is right with you now, and he will always be with you as you grow and dream and reach for the fullness of all he has called you to and created you to be.

But sometimes his calling on your life looks different than you imagine.

Bob wanted to be president of the United States when he was a kid. Instead, God planned for him to be the ADD kid who barely survived school but went on to start and lead a great one—Grace Prep. He loves it.

And Dannah wanted to be a vet or a missionary when she grew up. God's plan was for her to be a Bible teacher and author. She loves it, and his bonus to her is the farm, where she gets to be the vet to horses, llamas, goats, chickens, peacocks, and various other critters!

We both agree that God's plan is better in every way. Let him be the North Star of *your* life. He will lead you the best way.

Talk with Dad about the following questions and about God's plan for his life—and yours.

■ Ask your dad what he wanted to grow up to be when he was a kid. Write down his answer:

_____

_____

_____

_____

_____

■ And where has God led him now?
  Was it what he expected?

■ Where do you think God will lead you?
  Write it down (you may be surprised when you are an adult): _____

_____

_____

_____

Step 5: Finish Strong

Pray a prayer of surrender for yourself, and pray that your daughter would learn to follow God's guidance in her life. Let her pray too. End on a note of excitement for her future.

Challenge activity: A Celebration Date with Mom and Dad

Key verses: Ephesians 5:31-32

Objective: To begin to view marriage as a picture of God's love for his people

Materials needed: A reservation at a restaurant near you, a few index cards, a pencil or pen—and most important, her mom!

Step 1: Prep Talk

As this book comes out, Dannah and I will be celebrating 25 years of marriage. We are more in love than ever. Those hard times of separation and learning to love each other better have paid off big.

One of our simplest anniversary celebrations was the day that I surprised Dannah after chapel at Grace Prep with a re-creation of our first date. She was a cheap date. Little Caesars breadsticks and a couple of Wendy's Frosties at a public park were all it took to begin to win her heart. This time, to celebrate our marriage and evoke the romance of that first date I surprised her with 60 Frosties and 60 bags of breadsticks—one for each student in the school. (In case you need to know: an order this size has to be pre-arranged.) Who's to say that romance disappears over time? With effort it grows as the marriage relationship deepens.

At this point in her life, your daughter has taken "Mom and Dad" for granted. (Well, maybe yours never has, but mine both did from time to time.) This is a good thing. She takes you for granted because you've been steady and faithful. Always there. She is positively affected when she is around a Christ-centered marriage, but she probably hasn't thought much about it. While her heart is naturally inclined toward romance, it is still only a vague concept to her, and she probably doesn't know that you romanced a woman right out of her mind to bring her to be your wife. It's time to put things on the record for her. This date is your chance to share a glimpse into your marriage and love story with her in a fun way.

MOVIE ENCORE!

For an extra-special movie bonus, watch your wedding video together.

A touching father-daughter-marriage movie is *Father of the Bride*—either the blast from the past with Spencer Tracy or the newer version with Steve Martin.

In her book *Strong Fathers, Strong Daughters*, Dr. Meg Meeker has an entire chapter titled "Be the Man You Want Her to Marry." A simple point, but profound.

You want your daughter to marry a man of courage and integrity, loyalty and love, strength and honesty? Model that for her. She will see those times when you treat your wife like a queen, put your family first, and strive to do the right thing. She will respect you for it and expect nothing less from the man she will marry.

PLANNING DATE #7
Dress for Success

This simple dress-up date challenge is sure to be a hit with Dad, Mom, and daughter. Girls love to be romanced and made to feel special, even at the age of eight or ten. So pamper her by encouraging her to wear her favorite fancy dress and dressing up yourself. Maybe Mom can do your daughter's hair in a special style or let her use a little splash of perfume. Choose and make a reservation at a classy restaurant. Be sure to order an appetizer and dessert—nothing says a fancy meal like having three courses!

Consider personalizing your date. Into music? Take her to a hip eatery with live music. Love plays or musicals? Go to a less fancy place and save your bucks to take her to a show after dinner. Still live in the town where you fell in love? Choose a restaurant that has sentimental value to you and your wife.

1. Read through the rest of the date.

2. Make reservations at the fancy restaurant of your choice.

3. Tell both your wife and your daughter several days in advance so they have time to plan what to wear.

4. Remember to bring index cards, pens or pencils, and this book with you to the restaurant.

BUDGET CRUNCHER

If going out to a fancy restaurant is not feasible for you, transform your own dining room into a romantic spot. Use fine china and a linen tablecloth and linen napkins, and light a few candles. Turn on some elegant music. This evening is about your daughter, so arrange playdates for her siblings if possible. Prepare a nice meal, perhaps her favorite (no mac and cheese, though!), and have a fun dessert. One idea for a special dessert is to purchase a couple of gourmet cupcakes to share.

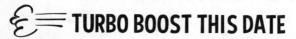 ## TURBO BOOST THIS DATE

There are a couple of ways to take this date to the gentle-man—I mean super-gentleman—level. Try any of the following suggestions.

Bring your wife and your daughter flowers before the date.

Tell Mom and daughter about the date a few days in advance and suggest they both get new outfits for it (this one is sure to make Mom feel special too).

Give your daughter a memento from your wedding, like a program or a dried flower from Mom's bouquet.

Pray for her future husband together.

Bring along any materials that tell your love story (handwritten notes, pictures, wedding album).

Step 2: SKG Radio for Your Ride to the Challenge

Play *Date #8: Dress for Success* during the car ride to the restaurant.

Step 3: Dad-Daughter Challenge

Your daughter will always remember this date. Guaranteed. She probably won't remember what she ate or the games she played, but she will remember that you took the time to share a very special part of your lives with her: your marriage.

PREP FOR LIFE

Chivalry is one of those qualities that are unfortunately slowly fading out of our culture. Teaching your daughter to look for respect and courtesy in a guy is something you can start to do now. On this date see how many ways you can show her (and your wife) a little of this old-fashioned virtue. Open the car and the restaurant door for them, drop them off so they don't have to walk through the parking lot in their nice clothes, and pull out their chairs for them. Chivalry is not condescending, as some feminists claim; rather, it's the first level of respect a guy can show a girl.

Step 4: Talk with Dad

Start your evening with a fun little game while you wait for your dinner (or play it after dessert—you don't have to be too structured).

Who Knows Me?

This one plays out something like the old *Newlywed Game*. Your daughter will read the questions and you and your wife will write down on your own cards (or napkins if you forgot the cards) what you think the other's response will be and your own answer to the question. You score points each time you correctly match your spouse's response. (Dad, I hope we don't get you into too much trouble here.)

For an example, look at the following:

Lexi reads the question: *"What's your favorite restaurant?"*

On his card Bob writes: *"Bob—Outback Steakhouse. Dannah—Little Caesars."*

On her card Dannah writes: *"Dannah—Olive Garden. Bob—Outback Steakhouse."*

Dannah scores one point for correctly identifying Bob's favorite restaurant. Bob loses a point for being cheap and realizes that now he has to spring for dessert.

We realize that Mom and Dad may not both be on this date. The game will work just as well played between Dad and daughter or Mom and daughter.

"Who Knows Me?" Questions:

What's your favorite restaurant?

What's your favorite movie?

Would you rather be able to be invisible or able to read minds?

What's your favorite meal?

What's your favorite color?

What's your favorite Bible character?

Would you rather be a famous singer or a famous movie star?

If you could only have one superpower, what would it be?

What is/was your favorite subject in school?

Would you rather be able to stop time or fly?

If you could travel anywhere in the world where would it be?

What would be your ideal pet?

If you could go back in time, where would you go?

What color shoes are you wearing right now?

If you could be in a movie, which would it be?

What is your favorite breakfast food?

Complete the rest of the Talk with Dad (and Mom) time after dinner. Pull out "Date #8: Dress for Success" from the Talk with Dad Pullouts in the back of this book. Give them to your daughter and talk through them, giving her time to fill in the blanks.

Talk with Dad
Dress for Success:
God's Wonderful Plan for Marriage

Remember, the following section is a copy of what we created for your daughter. It was written by Dannah and Suzanna for your girl. Turn to page 173 for the pullout version your daughter will use for this date.

Let your daughter try the True Love Matching activity in her pullout pages. Help her out if she needs it.

Everyone knows that fairy tales end with the words "and they lived happily ever after"! Let's see if you can match the true-love couples together:

True Love Matching

1. Superman — Rebekah

2. Prince Charming — The spoon

3. Gilbert — Maria

4. Prince William — Lois Lane

5. Adam — Duchess Catherine

6. Professor Bhaer — Cinderella

7. George Washington — Eve

8. Jacob — Jo (from *Little Women*)

9. The dish — Anne of Green Gables

10. Captain von Trapp — Martha Custis

Guess what? True love was God's idea! He designed marriage love to be a lasting, ride-into-the-sunset kind of love. He himself said, *"Love never fails"* (1 Corinthians 13:8 NASB). While falling in love and romance are wonderful (in fact, there is a whole book of the Bible centered on a man and a woman who are in love), marriage is about a lot more than just living "happily ever after" together.

> *"A man shall leave his father and his mother and hold fast to his wife, and the two shall become one flesh."*
>
> Ephesians 5:31

Isn't it amazing that God designed two people to become so close to one another that they "become one"? When a man and a woman marry, they promise to love and cherish each other for the rest of their lives. This is a promise to love the other person more than yourself, to always care for and honor them. Marriage requires both the husband and wife to be unselfish. Which can be hard…but the rewards of unselfish, giving love are deep and lasting.

Let's continue to the next verse.

> *"'…and the two shall become one flesh.' This mystery is profound, and I am saying that it refers to Christ and the church."*
>
> Ephesians 5:31-32

The glory of marriage is that it is designed to be a reflection of divine love! Jesus loved his bride, the church, so much that he died so that he could be close to her and bring her to heaven forever. And we, as the bride of Christ, are called to love Jesus first, before anything or anyone else. Wow—a husband and wife are called to be a picture of the gospel, which is the Good News from God to us!

*"Husbands, love your wives, as Christ loved the church
and gave himself up for her."*

Ephesians 5:25

*"Wives, submit to your own husbands, as to the Lord.
For the husband is the head of the wife even as Christ
is the head of the church."*

Ephesians 5:22-23

These verses tell us that the husband is called to love his
wife like Jesus loved the church, sacrificing everything for her.
The wife is called to be like the church, following her husband's
leadership and giving him her love.

*Your daughter will now have the opportunity to ask you
and your wife some questions about your love story. Be prepared to share lots of details. Your daughter will love all of the
nitty-gritty particulars like if you were nervous when you proposed, what song you danced to on your wedding day, and
what you were thinking when your wife-to-be walked down
the aisle. Be sure to tell her some fun and funny facts unique
to your romance.*

Step 5: Finish Strong

Take the opportunity to pray over your daughter together.
You could ask God to bless her with an amazing marriage (far
in the future), pray that your marriage would be an example of
God's love to her, and speak blessings over her.

PART 3

Other Great Stuff

Father-Daughter Devotional Challenge
Ideas for Single Moms
Talk with Dad Pullouts

Father-Daughter Devotional Challenge

BY SUZANNA D'SOUZA

We asked our writing partner, Suzanna, to create these devos for you and your daughter. She's a girl. So she thinks like one. And your daughter is going to love these tidbits of Scripture and stories that teach her how to build a disciplined prayer life. Dannah and I do!

—Bob

Day 1

In His Presence

"When Jesus had cried out again in a loud voice, he gave up his spirit. At that moment the curtain of the temple was torn in two from top to bottom."

Matthew 27:50-51

Before Jesus came to the earth, God's people worshipped him in the temple in the city of Jerusalem. The temple was similar to a church building, but it had several crucial differences. One difference was that there was a room for God in the temple that only the High Priest (kind of like the lead pastor of Israel) could enter. And even he was only allowed in once a year. This room was filled with the holy and glorious presence of God and was separated from the rest of the temple by a tall, thick curtain. This curtain was not like the drapes covering your front window—it was huge! It was 60 feet tall (that's taller than your house) and about half as wide.

This curtain represented sin. Sin separated us from God. We simply could not get close to him because he is pure and holy and we were not.

Then Jesus came to earth.

When Jesus died for our sins, the curtain in the temple was ripped in two, completely. Now anyone could go into the special room filled with God's presence. Jesus' death and resurrection washed our sins away (as long as we accept him as our Savior) so that we are now holy and pure children of God.

Just think about it for a second. The creator of the stars and moon wanted to be your Dad so much that he sacrificed his own Son to get rid of sin—the one thing separating us from him. Now that's love!

Before the curtain was torn, God only spoke to a few people, the priests and prophets. Now all of us can hear his voice if we listen. Reading the Bible, talking to him in prayer, and listening to the still, small voice of the Holy Spirit in our hearts are all ways that we can welcome his presence in our lives.

Live It

Read your favorite Bible verse together. What is God telling you through it?

Take some time now to talk and listen to God. Close your eyes and tell him what's on your mind. Try to listen to what he is saying to you. His voice may sound like a soft whisper in your heart, or you may feel the gentle peace of his presence.

Day 2
Take Time for God

"Seek first the kingdom of God and his righteousness."

Matthew 6:33

Breakfast, school, lunch, more school, soccer practice, piano lessons, dinner, playing with friends and siblings...bedtime. Life can get pretty busy sometimes, even for a kid! Sometimes the only time we leave for God during our busy weeks is church on Sunday mornings.

God wants to have a relationship with you. You and your dad have a special relationship as father and daughter. You and your mom have a special relationship as mother and daughter. What would happen, though, if you never spent any *time* with your parents? You wouldn't know them very well, would you? Think about a quirky thing that your dad does. You probably wouldn't know this if you hadn't spent any time together. It's the same with God. To know him, you have to make spending time with him an important part of your day.

If anyone could say they were too busy to spend time with God, it was Susanna Wesley. Susanna gave birth to 19 children and was a wise and good mother. As you can imagine, she was busy from the moment the sun rose to when it set at night. (How many pancakes do you think that family could eat on a Saturday morning?) Even though it would have been easy for her to make excuses for not spending time with God, Susanna never did. Sometimes she could only spare a few moments in the middle of her day. When that happened she would stop right where she was, put her apron over her head, and talk to him.

If Susanna could make time to talk to God, anyone can!

Live It

Think of the day of the week you are the busiest—maybe you have activities and homework after school. (Dad, you can do this too.) Write down a time when you can take a few moments (it doesn't have to be an hour) to be in God's presence on that day. Talk to him, read a few verses of Scripture, pray for friends and family members.

Day 3
All These Things

"I tell you, do not worry about your life, what you will eat or drink; or about your body, what you will wear. Is not life more than food, and the body more than clothes? Look at the birds of the air; they do not sow or reap or store away in barns, and yet your heavenly Father feeds them...For the pagans run after all these things, and your heavenly Father knows that you need them. But seek first his kingdom and his righteousness, and all these things will be given to you as well."

Jesus, in Matthew 6:25-26, 32-33

About 150 years ago in England lived a man who loved God with all of his heart. George Mueller was a preacher and pastor. He also loved people and decided to open up an orphanage to care for many parentless children who didn't have a home. The children were happy and healthy in the orphanage. Even though he was a poor preacher and didn't have much money, George had faith that God would provide for all of their needs.

One night there was no more food in the orphanage, nor

money to buy any. The children slept peacefully in their beds not knowing that the pantry was empty. Early in the morning George woke up and went for a walk to pray. On his walk he met an acquaintance who unexpectedly gave him some money. George thanked him and thanked Father God for providing money just at the right moment. The children woke up to a hot breakfast! George was not surprised that money appeared right when he needed it. He knew that God answered prayers and cared about each of those children.

Isn't it good to know that God cares about all of your needs? He cares about your spirit, soul, and body. He gives spiritual food for your spirit and soul (Jesus is sometimes called the "Bread of Life") and also cares about whether you have food and shelter for your body. Sometimes God provides by giving your parents jobs. Other times God provides in miraculous ways like he did with George.

Look and ask for miracles in your life. Sometimes the miracles are little blessings right under your nose. For instance, recently one young couple had car trouble. Money was tight because the husband was in school. But they did have $200 put aside in their car fund. After they took their car to the mechanic he said that it would cost $370 to get it fixed. He started to work on it. After a few hours he called the husband and said that the problem was not as bad as he thought. The final amount to get it fixed? Well—$198, $2 less than the money the couple had set aside!

You don't have to think about grown-up things like fixing your car. But thank your heavenly Father for meeting your needs. Look for little miracles in your life that show he takes care of you (maybe you made it into that special science club at school, maybe Mom and Dad got a tax refund, which paid for you to go to summer camp).

Live It

Thank God for providing for all of your needs. (Thank your dad and mom too—they work hard!) Make a list together of all of the things you are thankful for. If you and your family have physical needs ask God to provide for them.

Often God uses other people to provide for people's needs. Someone gave George the money for the orphans, after all. What is a way you can bless another person who maybe doesn't have as much as you do? Make it your mission this week to do it.

Day 4
Following the Lion

"He guides me along the right paths for his name's sake."

Psalm 23:3

Four children and one dwarf were lost in the woods, desperately trying to reach the camp of their friend, a prince in need of their help. The youngest of the bunch, a small nine-year-old girl, looked up between a few of the tall trees. There she saw him! Their savior, a lion named Aslan.

Prince Caspian is the second book in the beloved series The Chronicles of Narnia by C.S. Lewis. In this scene of the book, none of Lucy's fellow travelers see Aslan or believe that she saw him. Instead of listening to Lucy and following the lion's lead, they continue on the way they think is best and are nearly killed by arrows from their enemies.

A remarkable thing begins to happen once the children and dwarf decide to follow Lucy (who is following Aslan). None of them can see the lion at first. But then Lucy's brother Edmund says,

"Look! What's that shadow crawling down in front of us?"

"It's his shadow," said Lucy.

"I do believe you're right, Lu," said Edmund. "I can't think how I didn't see it before. But where is he?"

"With his shadow of course. Can't you see him?"

"Well, I almost thought I did—for a moment. It's such a rum light."[25]

As their journey continues and the travelers have more and more faith that Aslan is really leading them to safety, each one gradually starts to see him walking in front of them in the moonlight. He continues to lead them until they arrive at the camp of Prince Caspian, just in time to save the day.

Just like this wonderful story, following the lead of our Father God requires trust and faith. There are times when the right way to go is clear, like it was to Lucy. Everyone else says she is crazy, that she is seeing things. God's road sometimes seems out of the ordinary, and is not the way everyone else is going. In the story, Lucy chose to go with the others, *even though she knew that they were not going in the right direction*. What would have happened if she had decided to follow Aslan right away? The story doesn't tell us. But it does tell us what happened when she did make the decision to follow him.

If you know God's Word, then you have a pretty good idea of how to follow him with your actions and choices. It may be difficult (especially if your friends all think you are crazy), but his way is *always* better!

Or maybe you can't see God clearly at first, like the other children couldn't see Aslan. Sometimes God leads his children on a path that doesn't seem to make sense to you or anybody else. *Trusting* in God's guidance can be scary at first. However, *faith* grows (just like the children beginning to see Aslan) as God's children take more and more steps after him. That tentative first step turns into a second and a third; then a cautious walk turns into a confident stride, which grows into a jog and then a full-speed run. As you *trust* your present and your future to him and see that his path is good, your *faith* will increase. Then it becomes easy to see and follow him.

Live It

Think back over today (or yesterday). What was a way you showed trust in God through a choice you made? What was a choice you made to go your own direction? Discuss ways you can choose to follow God in your life.

Day 5
Sons of God

"You are all sons of God through faith in Christ Jesus."

Galatians 3:26 NKJV

On Monday morning you wake up hungry. Throwing your slippers on as you jump out of bed, you run down the steps to the refrigerator or cupboard. Grabbing an apple or bowl of cereal you plop down on a kitchen chair and begin to munch.

Did you know that you are welcome to "gobble up an apple" in God's kitchen? You are his son, after all. Wait a minute— *son?* Paul writes to the Galatians (a group of Jesus followers who lived in a city named Galatia) that "you are all sons of God." Even the girls. God called his children "sons" because back in the days when the Bible was written, being a son meant *you inherited all of the land, money, animals, and houses from Dad.*

That's right—those apples in the refrigerator? Yours. The goat in the backyard? Yours. The jar full of quarters? Yours.

Okay, so maybe you don't have a goat in the backyard. But grab ahold of the idea that everything that is God's, he has given to you too. While he has given us humans the earth to take care of (and that is really important), God also gives us love, joy, peace, patience, kindness, goodness, faithfulness, gentleness, and self-control. He is all of those qualities, and he wants you to have them too. He actually asks you to imitate him!

There are many times when we aren't loving and are impatient or selfish. Or maybe we find ourselves in a frustrating situation. In those times we have to let God love through us. We can ask him for his patience and let him help us control ourselves. As his children, he gives us peace that passes all understanding, love that never fails, and self-control that enables us to forgive our enemies.

Live It

Write two qualities you want to be known for (kindness, love…). Ask God to give you an extra dose of those qualities this week.

Day 6
Beautiful Feet

"How beautiful upon the mountains are the feet of him who brings good news, who proclaims peace, who brings glad tidings of good things, who proclaims salvation, who says to Zion, 'Your God reigns!'"

Isaiah 52:7

The Bible says that those who bring good news have *beautiful feet*. They have beautiful feet because wherever these people go, peace, good news, and joy go with them.

Everyone loved the sound of Edith Burns's footsteps. She told anyone she met about the best news of all: Jesus.

No matter if it was Thanksgiving, Christmas, or the Fourth of July, Edith always introduced herself by saying, "Hello, my name is Edith Burns. Do you believe in Easter?" Then she would tell them about how Jesus loved them so much that he came to the earth to die and be resurrected for them. Many, many people she talked to came to follow Jesus and become children of God.

One day, Edith went to see her doctor. She was Dr. Phillips' favorite patient, but that day he did not have good news for her. He told her sadly that she had cancer and would not live very much longer. Edith replied, "Why, Will Phillips, shame on you. Why are you so sad? Do you think God makes mistakes? You have just told me I'm going to see my precious Lord Jesus, my husband, and my friends. You have just told me that I am going to celebrate Easter forever, and here you are having difficulty giving me my ticket!" Instead of crying about the news, she was overjoyed.

Most people would say that Edith deserved a rest, to think about herself for a change instead of constantly thinking about other people and telling them the good news of Jesus. She did not stop telling people about Jesus, however. She even had a special request for God. She asked him to not take her to heaven until the head nurse in the hospital, Phyllis Cross, became a part of God's family. Phyllis was, well, rather cross and didn't want anything to do with God, and she told Edith so. Still, Edith did not give up on her. Every day, even in the midst of her own pain, she would tell the nurse that God loved her and that she was praying for her. Sure enough, one day, Phyllis came to Edith's room and asked Edith to tell her about Easter. She prayed and invited Jesus into her heart.

Edith Burns was known as "Easter Edith" because she spread the good news of Jesus wherever her feet carried her. What are you known for? Do people listen for your footsteps?

Live It

Telling people about the good news is important to God. As a loving Father he wants to welcome everyone into his family!

Write down a few ways that your feet can carry good news to those around you. How can you tell about God's love through your words and what you do? Choose one person to pray for this week who does not know Jesus.

Day 7
Tough Stuff

"Two are better than one, because they have a good return for their labor: if either of them falls down, one can help the other up."

Ecclesiastes 4:9-10

Imagine an obstacle course that lasts 12 miles and has over 20 challenges, like crawling in mud under barbed wire, swimming in ice-cube-cold water, and climbing over 20-foot walls. Sounds tough (and a little crazy)! Such races are becoming more and more popular. There is a curious thing about these races, though—they are not really "races," because the participants help each other through the course. In one event, at the starting line they even have to solemnly promise to help each other through the challenges. Teamwork is emphasized, and for a reason. No one would get very far, let alone finish, a course like this by themselves.

Just like in this obstacle course, life requires teamwork. God created us to rely on each other and help each other along. There are a few ways two can be better than one.

God created us to need mentors—older people who can help us grow in our faith (like Dad). Even grown-ups need mentors, like a pastor, who will give words of advice.

By surrounding yourself with friends who love God, you can encourage each other to grow in his ways. One day you may have a special partner in your husband, who you will walk beside. Right now, make sure you have some friends who love God.

You can also *be* a mentor. God has already taught you things and spoken to you. Even helping a little one (maybe your brother or sister) learn how to share or practice self-control is passing on his wisdom. Another way you can be a mentor is to help out at church. Remember, being a mentor is not about being bossy but about showing God's love.

The apostle Paul addressed fellow Christians as "brothers and sisters" in his letters. Once you have accepted Jesus into your heart you have become a part of God's family. And families help each other. Don't be a Lone Ranger. (And even the Lone Ranger needed his friend Tonto!)

Live It

Write down who you think your mentors are. Make a point of asking them for advice and going to them with your problems or questions about God.

Write down who you think your godly gal pals are. How do you help each other?

Write down the name of a younger person (or younger people) you can help teach God's ways.

Ideas for Single Moms

BY DANNAH

A s a single mom, you are all too familiar with the struggle to be both mom and dad to your children. You are not alone! According to the U.S. Census Bureau, 24 percent of children under 18 live with only their mother. That's almost one in four kids. Another 3.5 percent of kids live with only their dad. [26] Despite the fact that so many children are growing up in single-parent households, this is rarely addressed in a helpful or positive manner in our society.

Let's face it—as a church and a culture we have done a miserable job in easing the many challenges you face as a single parent. We have often been quick to ignore your situation, pass judgment, or solemnly spout statistics rather than provide emotional and practical support. Hopefully you have found encouragement and helping hands in your community. If we could reach through these pages we would give you a hug and a hearty pat on the back. You have strength! We hope that this date manual will be a useful tool in helping you equip your daughter for life.

There has been a lot of focus on how fatherlessness affects sons but, by picking up this book, you've shown you realize that daughters also have a strong father hunger. Your little girl *needs* exposure to godly men in her life. A daughter heart naturally yearns for a connection to a father heart. If that need for affirmation and security is not met, your daughter will be more likely to turn to the wrong places to fill that void. Social and behavioral problems, lack of self-worth, teen promiscuity and pregnancy, and even poor academic performance have all been linked to fatherlessness.[27] Your daughter is also in danger of judging men and even God through the prism of her experience: *absent*. Mom, be proactive! We encourage you to seek out men, perhaps your father or brother, who could speak godly wisdom and encouragement to her.

The topics in this book are important to introduce now, while your girl's beliefs about what it means to be a woman, what it means to be a man, and how she should relate to boys are being formed. We know you are doing everything you can to provide a positive, loving environment for your daughter. But a woman simply can't communicate a *guy's perspective* of men, marriage, and masculinity. Only a man can do that! So invite a relative or godly family friend to go through these 8 Great Dates with you and your daughter. Be sure this is someone who has already developed a healthy, meaningful relationship with your children.

Excepting the dress-up date, these eight outings were designed to be adventures for only dad and daughter. This special, focused, one-on-one time promotes a healthy deepening of their relationship that wouldn't be as easy if mom were along. However, we strongly recommend that you join in on the activities and mission debriefing time with your daughter and the man (grandpa, uncle…) who is stepping up to this challenge. Take a backseat, particularly on the mission debriefing times (give the man a chance to talk), but be there. In the end, you are the one she will come to with questions and concerns.

Read through each date in the main section of the book, then take a look at our suggested modifications before planning each date.

Date #1: Mission Possible! This date is fairly straightforward and requires little change. Just go along for the ride.

Date #2: Sugar and Spice and Everything Nice. Try your best to stay out of the kitchen for this activity. Let your daughter and her "date" bake their treat together. Be on hand, though, in case they can't find an ingredient or a pan, for the debriefing time and, of course, to taste their creation!

Date #3: As You Wish. The focus of this date is comparing true love with counterfeit love. It doesn't require much modification. Enjoy the movie together!

Date #4: Sticks and Stones (or the "Italian Job"). Jesus addressed God as "Abba" (Daddy). This was revolutionary. In that time, God was viewed as someone to be feared, respected, and obeyed; he wasn't a tender, loving Father. But Jesus paved the way for us to be God's children. Your daughter can know God as her Daddy, even if her earthly daddy is not present in her life. This is probably the most important lesson she will ever learn! Mom, you have the awesome privilege of helping her to cultivate her relationship with her heavenly Father.

Enjoy the hike. Take a backseat during the mission debriefing time. Don't skip the Father–Daughter Devo Challenge— you can do it together. Better yet, begin working your way through *The One Year Mother–Daughter Devo,* Dannah's devotional. Developing a relationship with God takes place over time, so walk with her daily.

Date #5: Natural Treasure. It is powerful for a girl to hear her father say that she is a treasure because it boosts her self-esteem and gives her a profound sense of security. Every girl needs a knight in shining armor. Accordingly, please let the father figure in your daughter's life take the lead in affirming her value on this date, not you. (I'm sure you tell her she is a princess every day already.)

Participate in the treasure hunt. For a fun twist, hide the "treasure" in your purse or pocket (don't forget to change the last clue!).

Date #6: How Does Your Garden Grow? This date is all about letting God's Word help you grow. Be the activity facilitator for this date. After all, you and your daughter will be watching your seeds sprout or your plant grow together.

Date #7: Star Track—The Final Frontier. Let the guy take the lead on the techie and nerdy part of this date (we know you could do it just fine, but he will probably enjoy looking up star facts with which to astonish your daughter). Maybe you could scope out a location. Have fun stargazing together.

Date #8: Dress for Success. It is essential for your daughter to be exposed to a good, godly marriage on a regular basis. Especially since, for whatever reason, she isn't exposed to one in her home. This may be a painful subject for you to discuss, particularly since your daughter will probably ask you questions that may bring up a past full of hurt or sadness. So be prepared for her questions, but don't be discouraged. Your daughter will get excited about God's brilliant design for marriage. Guaranteed.

There are a few practical details you should consider. One option is to let the man who has been helping with these dates (if he is a relative) take his wife, you, and your daughter all out for dinner (this would work great with grandparents). If you so decide, your daughter can ask the marriage questions of them (how they met, and so on). Another option would be to make this a special mother–daughter date. Your girl will love spending time with you on this dress-up date. Take a few moments to share some of your own perspective on marriage with her and of your hope for her future. Pray together, just the two of you, after the date. Ask God to bless her future husband and to begin to prepare them both to have an incredible, love-filled, out-of-this-world marriage.

A Final Word

Every mom feels like she rarely has a free moment, so taking time for these dates is truly an investment, and maybe even a sacrifice. Don't feel guilty if you need to skip some or all of the Prep for Life or Turbo Boost suggestions. Save those ideas for another day, and when you get around to them maybe remind your daughter of the corresponding date. The goal of these dates is simply to invest in your daughter. So dive in and get started!

Just for You, God's

Secret Keeper GIRL

Talk with Dad Pullouts

Talk with Dad

Mission Possible!
Understanding Boys

Welcome to Secret Keeper Girl's 8 Great Dates for Dads and Daughters. You may have just committed your first practical joke! Congratulations. You took on the mission and successfully completed it. Another *possible* mission in life will be understanding boys!

Read Jeremiah 29:11 and fill in the blanks:

"'I know the _____ I have for you,' declares the LORD,

'_____ to prosper you and not to harm you,

_____ to give you hope and a future.'"

Jeremiah 29:11

Based on that verse, fill in this blank:

God has a _____ for my life.

He must also have a plan for the fact that boys are in your life. While that may not include marriage, it most likely will. God's plan for a girl in the Bible named Rebekah included marriage. She was a few years older than you when this story took place.

Rebekah was just an ordinary, everyday girl who was respectful of her parents. One day, while going about her daily task of getting water for her family, she met a visitor from a distant land who was in need of water for himself and his camels. Interested in the opportunity to meet someone from a land that she had only heard of, she offered to draw water from the well for the man and his animals. She could not have known that this simple act of service would change her life. The traveler she helped was actually Abraham's servant, who had been sent on an adventure of his own. He had been sent to locate a wife for the son of his master, Abraham, in the land of their origin. The servant's name was Eliezer, and he prayed to God for help in completing the mission Abraham had assigned to him. This is what he asked of God:

> "See, I am standing here beside this spring, and the young women of the town are coming out to draw water. This is my request. I will ask one of them, 'Please give me a drink from your jug.' If she says, 'Yes, have a drink, and I will water your camels, too!'—let her be the one you have selected as Isaac's wife. This is how I will know that you have shown unfailing love to my master."
>
> Genesis 24:13-14 NLT

Does his request sound familiar? Yes, because that's exactly what Rebekah did! By embracing and seeking out God's adventure for her life in her everyday activities, she was led to marry Abraham's son. She would become the grandmother of 12 young men. These young men would grow up to be the leaders of the 12 tribes that form the nation of Israel. And Rebekah? She would be the great, great, great, great, great, great, great (insert 30 more "greats")...grandmother of Jesus. And the beginning of this great adventure happened while she was doing her daily chores. (Think about that the next time your mom asks you to empty the dishwasher or take out the trash!)

—by Jarrod

God had a plan for Rebekah: to be one of the ancestors of Jesus!

And that plan included a boy named Isaac (who drove a really nice camel).

Not bad. Not bad at all.

Talk with Dad about the following questions and write your answers in the blanks as you discuss the *very possible* mission of understanding boys.

- Who do you think likes practical jokes better—boys or girls?

  _____

  _____

  _____

  _____

- What are some differences you've observed when you compare boys and girls?

  _____

  _____

  _____

  _____

- Why do you think God created boys and girls to be so different?

  _____

  _____

  _____

  _____

- What plans do you think God *might* have for your life?

_____

_____

_____

_____

- You probably won't find a husband by giving water to camels, but do you hope you'll be married one day? Why or why not?

_____

_____

_____

_____

_____

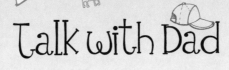

Talk with Dad

Sugar and Spice and Everything Nice: Understanding Girls

What amazing dessert did you and your dad just make? Draw a picture of it in the box below.

Dessert with Dad

To better understand how God has created boys and what makes them different, you need to understand how God has crafted and wired you. What makes you unique? Did you know that just like the special recipe that you prepared with your dad, your heavenly Father has a special recipe just for you? It's a top-secret recipe he has only used once, and that was when he made you. There is only one you, and there will never ever be anyone just like you. In the recipe card below, list some of the "ingredients" God used to make you. Under "directions," write down a good thing you can do with each "ingredient."

Secret Keeper GIRL

Recipe For _____

INGREDIENTS	DIRECTIONS

God created you to be marvelously unique and special. He made you a girl, who will grow into a woman. Do you know how wonderful that is? One chapter of the Bible honors an especially good example of womanhood. She is known as the "Proverbs 31 woman." Not all women will be like her, because Proverbs 31 is not a chapter with commands for what a woman *must* be, but an example of what a really exceptional woman *can* be.

Look at the verses below. With your dad, read each section out loud and then write an "ingredient" like "strength" or "hard-working" that describes what you just read.

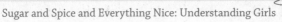

Verses 10-12

A wife of noble character who can find? She is worth far more than rubies. Her husband has full confidence in her and lacks nothing of value. She brings him good, not harm, all the days of her life.

Ingredient: _____

Verses 13-15

She selects wool and flax and works with eager hands. She is like the merchant ships, bringing her food from afar. She gets up while it is still night; she provides food for her family.

Ingredient: _____

Verses 16-17

She considers a field and buys it; out of her earnings she plants a vineyard. She sets about her work vigorously; her arms are strong for her tasks.

Ingredient: _____

Verse 20

She opens her arms to the poor and extends her hands to the needy.

Ingredient: _____

Verses 24-25

She makes linen garments and sells them, and supplies the merchants with sashes. She is clothed with strength and dignity; she can laugh at the days to come.

Ingredient: _____

Verses 26-29

She speaks with wisdom, and faithful instruction is on her tongue. She watches over the affairs of her household and does not eat the bread of idleness. Her children arise and call her blessed; her husband also, and he praises her: "Many women do noble things, but you surpass them all."

Ingredient: _____

Verse 30

Charm is deceptive, and beauty is fleeting; but a woman who fears the Lord is to be praised.

Ingredient: _____

Talk with Dad about the following questions and write your answers together.

- When was the last time your mom picked up some wool and flax or made linen garments? What does your mom do instead that would be like that?

- How could we rewrite some of these verses to describe a modern-day Proverbs 31 woman?

- What can you do to look like a Proverbs 31 girl?

  _____

  _____

- In the space below, work with your dad to make a list of the ingredients you want to have as a godly girl:

  _____   _____

  _____   _____

  _____   _____

  _____   _____

Talk with Dad

As You Wish:
True Love vs. Counterfeit Love

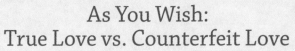

True love. It took Buttercup awhile to realize it, but when Westley was saying, "As you wish" what he meant was "I love you." The narrator goes on to tell us that what was even more amazing was the day she realized she loved him back. True love was born.

The Bible describes true love in 1 Corinthians 13:4-8:

> *"Love is patient, love is kind. It does not envy, it does not boast, it is not proud. It does not dishonor others, it is not self-seeking, it is not easily angered, it keeps no record of wrongs. Love does not delight in evil but rejoices with the truth. It always protects, always trusts, always hopes, always perseveres. Love never fails."*

A friend of mine once suggested that I replace every reference to the word *love* in that passage with my name, as a test to see how good I was at true love. Let's try it. Insert your name in the blanks below. (And consider how true the sentence ends up being.)

True Love Test

_____ is patient,

_____ is kind.

_____ does not envy,

_____ does not boast,

_____ is not proud.

_____ does not dishonor others,

_____ is not self-seeking,

_____ is not easily angered,

_____ keeps no record of wrongs.

_____ does not delight in evil
          but rejoices with the truth.

_____ always protects, always trusts,
          always hopes, always perseveres.

_____ never fails.

How did you do? (Hopefully you did a little better than I did the first time I tried it!) You can use this same test with others when you think they may be trying to sell you a counterfeit. Let me be specific. As you get older, boys are going to start to notice how beautifully God has created you and they are going to start to compete for your attention.

Some boys will offer you false love.

These boys will be the opposite of 1 Corinthians 13. Over time you'll see that they are untruthful, selfish, impatient, unkind, boastful, proud, dishonoring of others, easily angered, and all that other stuff. Run from them.

Some boys will carry with them a heart for true love.

These boys will be able to fill their name in the blanks and the sentences will be true.

A boy who offers you true love might be a little like Westley. What was the sentence he always spoke to Buttercup?

> "As _____ _____."

In this way, he was putting her ahead of his own desires. He was really saying, "I love you."

Talk with Dad about the following questions and write your answers in the blanks as you discuss what true love looks like.

- How hard do you think it is to grow into expressing true love?

  _____

  _____

  _____

- What kinds of things might a boy who is offering you fake love ask for?

  _____

  _____

  _____

- Who do you know who is an example of true love?

  _____

  _____

  _____

  _____

- How did you do in the 1 Corinthians True Love Test? What areas do you need to work on improving?

  _____

  _____

  _____

  _____

Talk with Dad

Sticks and Stones (or the "Italian Job"): God's Masterpiece

"Yes, my soul, find rest in God;
My hope comes from Him.
Truly He is my rock and my salvation;
He is my fortress, I will not be shaken."

Psalm 62:5-6

On your hike today you and your dad found seven rocks. Each one has a special meaning you are going to talk about with your dad now as you draw or trace them and record what they represent.

Talk with Dad about the rocks you collected. Make drawings or tracings of them and fill in the blanks as you discuss how God made you to be his unique daughter.

The Big Rock

It represents: _____

The Smooth Rock

It represents: _____

The Round Rock

It represents: _____

The Broken Rock

It represents: _____

The Smallest Rock

It represents: _____

The Colored Rock

It represents: _____

The Unique Rock

It represents: _____

Your value comes from God. Not from anyone or anything else. He made you to be unique—one of a kind—just like the rock you found on your hike. And he wants to continue to mold and shape you into the person he has created you to be. You can trust him to always be there for you, to be your rock.

It's exciting to be a daughter of God!

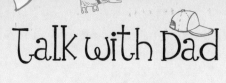

⑤ Talk with Dad

Natural Treasure: Learning My Value

In 1980, a man named Kevin Hillier took his metal detector out for a walk near the town of Kingower in Australia. Imagine his excitement when he found a gold nugget! And not

just any gold nugget—this shiny piece of metal weighs 61 pounds and is the largest known gold nugget in existence. Its name is the Hand of Faith (in my opinion, it looks like a bullfrog if viewed sideways!).

Gold, silver, pearls, emeralds, diamonds, rubies. Such precious metals and gems have long been sought by treasure hunters. But do you know what is more valuable than all of the gold and diamonds found in the earth? You! In fact, God not only knows what color hair you have, he knows *how many hairs* you have on your head.[28] In his eyes, you are precious. In your dad's eyes, you are precious. One day your husband will think you are precious and will tell you he loves you more than anyone in the world.

Let's look at Proverbs 31:10 again. It says, *"A wife of noble character who can find? She is worth far more than rubies."*

What woman, if she had a beautiful diamond necklace, would wear it to dig in the garden or while she was going swimming? When something is precious we treat it well and take care of it. How much more should you take care of *you*? Let's look at some ways that you can treat yourself like a treasure.

Talk with Dad about the following verses and questions and take some time to fill in the blanks.

1. Body

"Do you not know that your bodies are temples of the Holy Spirit, who is in you, whom you have received from God?" (1 Corinthians 6:19).

Treasure—what's a good way to take care of your body?

_____

_____

Trash—what's a way you can disrespect your body?

_____

_____

2. Emotions

"Above all else, guard your heart [inner part, mind, will, emotions], for everything you do flows from it" (Proverbs 4:23).

Treasure—what's a good way you can use your emotions?

_____

_____

Trash—what's a bad way you can use your emotions?

_____

_____

3. Thoughts

"Whatever is true, whatever is noble, whatever is right, whatever is pure, whatever is lovely, whatever is admirable—if anything is excellent or praiseworthy—think about such things" (Philippians 4:8).

Treasure—what are some good thoughts to dwell on?

_____

_____

Trash—what are some bad thoughts to dwell on?

_____

_____

4. Time

"Be very careful, then, how you live—not as unwise but as wise, making the most of every opportunity" (Ephesians 5:15).

Treasure—what's a good way to spend your time?

_____

_____

Trash—what's a bad way to spend your time?

_____

_____

5. Energy

"'Love the Lord your God with all your heart and with all your soul and with all your strength and with all your mind'; and 'Love your neighbor as yourself'" (Luke 10:27).

Treasure—what's a good thing to spend your energy on?

_____

_____

Trash—what's a bad thing to spend your energy on?

_____

_____

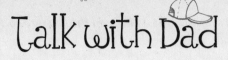

Talk with Dad

DATE #
6

How Does Your Garden Grow?
The Power of God's Word

What is a seed? How can a little acorn turn into a giant oak? Jesus told a story about some seeds once.

> *"What do you make of this? A farmer planted seed. As he scattered the seed, some of it fell on the road, and birds ate it. Some fell in the gravel; it sprouted quickly but didn't put down roots, so when the sun came up it withered just as quickly. Some fell in the weeds; as it came up, it was strangled by the weeds. Some fell on good earth, and produced a harvest beyond his wildest dreams."*
>
> *Matthew 13:3-8* MSG

In order for a seed to sprout, grow, and eventually bear fruit a lot of things need to happen. It has to survive being eaten (by birds, bunnies, squirrels, or even you). It has to have a place to grow (there is no place for roots to grow in gravel). It has to have space to grow (no weeds). Above all, it needs good soil and life giving water. But when it does grow it produces lots of delicious things to eat. Just think of how much of our food comes from those little seeds. Yum!

You might have guessed that Jesus wasn't just talking about seeds in his story. He goes on to explain that the seeds in the story are God's love, the gospel.

> *"When anyone hears news of the kingdom and doesn't take it in, it just remains on the surface, and so the Evil One comes along and plucks it right out of that*

person's heart. This is the seed the farmer scatters on the road.

The seed cast in the gravel—this is the person who hears and instantly responds with enthusiasm. But there is no soil of character, and so when the emotions wear off and some difficulty arrives, there is nothing to show for it.

The seed cast in the weeds is the person who hears the kingdom news, but weeds of worry and illusions about getting more and wanting everything under the sun strangle what was heard, and nothing comes of it.

The seed cast on good earth is the person who hears and takes in the News, and then produces a harvest beyond his wildest dreams."

Matthew 13:19-23 MSG

I don't know about you, but I want to be the person who lets the seed of God's love grow in my heart until it is as tall and strong as an apple tree. One of the best ways that will help us to grow is to read God's Word, the Bible.

Just for fun, let's try a quiz. If you don't know the answers, you and your dad can figure them out together.

Quick Bible Trivia Quiz

What is the longest book of the Bible?

Which person lived to be the oldest in the Bible?

How many books of the Bible share the story of Jesus (the Gospels)?

What three angels are mentioned by name in the Bible?

How many disciples did Jesus have?

How many books of the Bible are named after women?

What is the shortest verse in the Bible?

What are some of the instruments used to praise God in the Psalms?

What are the fruit of the Spirit? Can you name them all?

What's your favorite verse in the Bible?

Facts are fun, but remember this: as we read God's Word and spend time with him, his love will grow and produce fruit in us.

Talk with Dad about the following questions and how you can both grow in God's Word. Be sure to take the Father–Daughter Devo Challenge that follows.

- How has God's Word helped you grow already? (Hint: fruit of the Spirit)
- Why do you think that reading the Bible helps you grow?
- How often do you open God's Word and read it? Find a verse and commit it to memory this week.

Father–Daughter Devo Challenge

All right. It's time to get ready for some great God time together over the next several weeks. In this book are seven devotions for you to read together. Do one devo a week for seven weeks or go through all seven in one week. Choose what works best for you. Be sure, however, to set a day and time ahead of time to help keep you on track. Then just grab this book and jump right in! Start by reading the devotion aloud to each other.

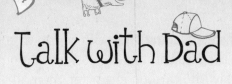

Talk with Dad

Star Track—The Final Frontier: Let God Be the North Star

*LORD, our Lord, how majestic is your name
in all the earth!
You have set your glory above the heavens.*

Psalm 8:1

Our God is an amazingly extravagant God. There are more stars than we are able to count—and yet in another verse God says that he counts all of the stars and knows them each by name. Isn't he incredible?

Looking into the night sky (don't use your phone yet) see if you can see any constellations. How about planets? The North Star, Polaris, is often mistaken as the brightest one in the sky. It's not, though. It actually ranks fiftieth in brightness.

To find the North Star you simply need to locate the Big Dipper (which is part of the constellation Ursa Major). The two outer stars of the Big Dipper's bowl point directly to Polaris. Polaris is also the last star in the handle of the Little Dipper (part of Ursa Minor). See if the two of you can spot it without technological help at first.

While all of the other stars in the night sky seem to change locations over time, Polaris just sits there night after night in the same spot. Should you ever find yourself lost in the dark, the North Star can be your guide out of the woods.

Enjoy exploring other constellations and planets using your phone app for help. (Funny fact: try pointing your phone at the ground to see what the sky looks like on the other side of the world.) Now try coming up with your own constellations. Maybe there is a group of stars that look like the outline of your pet or your favorite cartoon character. After all, that's pretty much what the Greeks did!

As I am sure you know, the planets in our solar system (including Earth) follow a path—an orbit—that circles the sun. The Earth's path is perfectly situated to allow for life to exist upon our little blue planet. If we were any closer to the sun we would burn up; any further and we would all be icicles. Isn't it wonderful that God placed the Earth on such a perfect path?

You are on a perfect path too. And God is right with you now, and he will always be with you as you grow and dream and reach for the fullness of all he has called you to and created you to be.

But sometimes his calling on your life looks different than you imagine.

Bob wanted to be president of the United States when he was a kid. Instead, God planned for him to be the ADD kid who barely survived school but went on to start and lead a great one—Grace Prep. He loves it.

And Dannah wanted to be a vet or a missionary when she grew up. God's plan was for her to be a Bible teacher and author. She loves it, and his bonus to her is the farm, where she gets to be the vet to horses, llamas, goats, chickens, peacocks, and various other critters!

We both agree that God's plan is better in every way. Let him be the North Star of *your* life. He will lead you the best way.

Talk with Dad about the following questions and about God's plan for his life—and yours.

- Ask your dad what he wanted to grow up to be when he was a kid. Write down his answer:

  _____

  _____

  _____

  _____

  _____

- And where has God led him now?
  Was it what he expected?

- Where do you think God will lead you?
  Write it down (you may be surprised when you are an adult): _____

  _____

  _____

  _____

Talk with Dad

Dress for Success:
God's Wonderful Plan for Marriage

Everyone knows that fairy tales end with the words "and they lived happily ever after"! Let's see if you can match the true-love couples together:

True Love Matching

1. Superman — Rebekah

2. Prince Charming — The spoon

3. Gilbert — Maria

4. Prince William — Lois Lane

5. Adam — Duchess Catherine

6. Professor Bhaer — Cinderella

7. George Washington — Eve

8. Jacob — Jo (from *Little Women*)

9. The dish — Anne of Green Gables

10. Captain von Trapp — Martha Custis

Guess what? True love was God's idea! He designed marriage love to be a lasting, ride-into-the-sunset kind of love. He himself said, *"Love never fails"* (1 Corinthians 13:8 NASB). While falling in love and romance are wonderful (in fact, there is a whole book of the Bible centered on a man and a woman who are in love), marriage is about a lot more than just living "happily ever after" together.

> *"A man shall leave his father and his mother and hold fast to his wife, and the two shall become one flesh."*
>
> *Ephesians 5:31*

Isn't it amazing that God designed two people to become so close to one another that they "become one"? When a man and a woman marry, they promise to love and cherish each other for the rest of their lives. This is a promise to love the other person more than yourself, to always care for and honor them. Marriage requires both the husband and wife to be unselfish. Which can be hard…but the rewards of unselfish, giving love are deep and lasting.

Let's continue to the next verse.

> *"'…and the two shall become one flesh.' This mystery is profound, and I am saying that it refers to Christ and the church."*
>
> *Ephesians 5:31-32*

The glory of marriage is that it is designed to be a reflection of divine love! Jesus loved his bride, the church, so much that he died so that he could be close to her and bring her to heaven forever. And we, as the bride of Christ, are called to love Jesus first, before anything or anyone else. Wow—a husband and wife are called to be a picture of the gospel, which is the Good News from God to us!

NOTES

1. This story is told in its entirety in a book entitled *Pursuing the Pearl: The Quest for a Pure, Passionate Marriage* (Chicago: Moody Publishers, 2002), which I wrote after we did finally yield to Christ's magnificent healing.

2. Felicia Paik, "Private Properties," The *Wall Street Journal*, July 2, 1999.

3. Meg Meeker, *Strong Fathers, Strong Daughters: 10 Secrets Every Father Should Know* (New York: Ballantine Books, 2006), 23.

4. Jane R. Dickie et al., "Parent-Child Relationships and Children's Images of God," *Journal for the Scientific Study of Religion* 36 (March 1997), 1.

5. Respectively, Revelation 19:6; Matthew 6:26.

6. Brennan Manning, *The Furious Longing of God* (Colorado Springs, CO: David C. Cook, 2009). From chapter titled "Our Father," Kindle edition.

7. Alex Kuczynski, "She's Got to Be a Macho Girl," The *New York Times*, November 3, 2002.

8. Kuczynski.

9. Kuczynski.

10. Dennis Rainey, *Aggressive Girls, Clueless Boys: 7 Conversations You Must Have With Your Son* (Little Rock, AR: Family Life Publishing, 2012), 16.

11. Crisis Connection, "Media Influence on Youth," Crisis Connection website, accessed October 21, 2013 at www.crisisconnectioninc.org/teens/media_influence_on_youth.htm.

12. American Psychological Association, "Sexualization of Girls," www.apa.org/pi/women/programs/girls/report.aspx.

13. Linda Nielsen, "College Daughters' Relationships with Their Fathers: A 15 year study," *College Student Journal*, Spring 2006.

14. Cheryl Wetzstein, "Youthful Indiscretion; Tweens' Pairing Up Worrisome," The *Washington Times*, February 27, 2008, retrieved 10/30/12 from www.highbeam.com/doc/1G1-175463078.html.

15. Joshua Mann, Joe S. McIlhaney Jr., and Curtis Stine, *Building Healthy Futures: Tools for Helping Adolescents Avoid or Delay the Onset of Sexual Activity* (Austin, TX: The Medical Institute for Sexual Health, 2000), p. 26.

16. Lynda G. Boothroyd and David I. Perrett, "Father Absence, Parent-Daughter Relationships and Partner Preferences," *Journal of Evolutionary Psychology* 6 (2008), 195.

17. Bruce J. Ellis et al., "Does Father Absence Place Daughters at Special Risk for Early Sexual Activity and Teenage Pregnancy?" *Child Development* 74:3 (2003), http://publicaccess.nih.gov/, retrieved on 10/29/12.

18. Ellis.

19. Ellis.

20. The Eating Disorder Foundation, "About Eating Disorders," retrieved 11/02/12 from www.eatingdisorderfoundation.org/EatingDisorders.htm.

21. Meeker, 70.

22. The Barna Group, "New Marriage and Divorce Statistics Released," March 31, 2008, retrieved 05/31/13 from www.barna.org/barna-update/article/15-familykids/42-new-mar riage-and-divorce-statistics-released.

23. Meeker, 190.

24. Matthew 10:30.

25. C.S. Lewis, *Prince Caspian* (New York: Macmillan Publishing Company, 1970), 145.

26. United States Census Bureau, "Families and Living Arrangements," table C3, 2011, retrieved 05/31/13 from www.census.gov/hhes/families/data/cps2011.html.

27. Edward Kruk, "Dads Needed on Father's Day," The *Washington Times,* June 15, 2012.

28. Matthew 10:30.

Also by Dannah Gresh

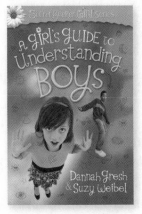

Secret Keeper Girl® Series
A GIRL'S GUIDE TO UNDERSTANDING BOYS
Coauthored by Suzy Weibel

Peer pressure and relationships with boys are really scary topics in mother-daughter relationships. That's why Dannah Gresh and Suzy Weibel take your daughter to the Bible as her resource, helping her meditate on its message and have fun while she does it. She'll explore questions like

- How come God made girls so that they like boys?
- Why are all my friends boy-crazy? Should *I* be?
- How can I stand out from others and be pure without losing my friends?

You'll love the biblical grounding and solid guidance that will help you with mother-daughter issues over boys—and help your daughter gain a foundation for godly relationships with young men.

Secret Keeper Girl® Series
SIX WAYS TO KEEP THE "LITTLE" IN YOUR GIRL
Guiding Your Daughter from Her Tweens to Her Teens

Today's world pressures girls to act older than they are when they're not ready for it. How can you help your tween daughter navigate the stormy waters of boy-craziness, modesty, body image, media, Internet safety, and more?

Dannah Gresh shares six easy ways to help your daughter grow up to be confident, emotionally healthy, and strong in her faith. In a warm and transparent style, Dannah shows you how to

- help your daughter celebrate her body in a healthy way
- unbrand her when the world tries to buy and sell her
- unplug her from a plugged-in world
- dream with her about her future

Six Ways to Keep the "Good" in Your Boy
Guiding Your Son from His Tweens to His Teens

God created boys to become men who are *good*—embracing God's call to unselfishly provide and protect. As a mom, you have a unique role in this process.

Dannah Gresh blends thorough analysis of the trends that can impact your son—including porn, aggressive girls, and video games gone overboard—with positive, practical advice any mom can use effectively to help guide her son toward "good" during the vital ages of 8 to 12. Dannah shows you

- why a boy needs to play outside
- how reading good books makes him a leader
- what role a mom plays in his entrance into manhood
- tips to keep him unplugged from impurity

----
*With special insights for dads from Bob Gresh
and for single moms from Angela Thomas*

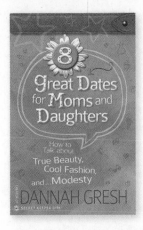

8 GREAT DATES FOR MOMS AND DAUGHTERS

How to Talk About True Beauty, Cool Fashion, and…Modesty!

"I wish Secret Keeper Girl had been available when our daughter was moving through her tweens. She and her mother would have loved sharing these 'great dates' together."

DR. JAMES DOBSON

One of the greatest protections against the culture's push to make your daughter mature too quickly is quality connecting time with you. Dannah Gresh has developed this new and updated "date" book with simple plans for eight fun activities to share (think facials, tea parties, shopping challenges!). Perfect for you and your energetic 8- to 12-year-old, each date helps you answer real-life questions like—

- "What is real beauty?"
- "How can I feel okay about my body?"
- "*Why* do I have to dress modestly?"
- "How do I take care of my hair?"

You'll find proven methods to bring up a healthy, grounded, and spiritually whole girl!

Need a guide to boys for the teen girl in your life?

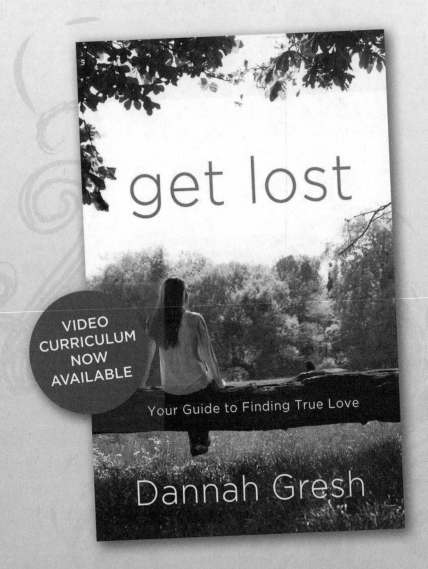

get lost

VIDEO CURRICULUM NOW AVAILABLE

Your Guide to Finding True Love

Dannah Gresh

Does the teen girl in your life suffer from boy-craziness? Help her discover how to get so lost in God that a guy has to seek Him to find her. Dannah Gresh traces God's language of love through Scripture to help a teen identify her true longings and let God answer them.

With a guided ten-day Love Feast Challenge, *Get Lost* has free video support online for small group study.

For more information go to www.dannahgresh.com.

What is a
Secret Keeper Girl?

Well, she's a lot of things. And she's NOT a lot of things. She's NOT a mean girl. She's a girl whose friendships are full of kindness. She's NOT boy crazy. (Moms, can we get an Amen?) She's a girl who knows she can share all of her heart-secrets with her mom at any time.

She's also a girl who embraces modesty. Why? Because she knows that she is a masterpiece created by God. She strives to keep the deepest secrets of her authentic beauty a secret! Maybe you are new to our movement, or maybe you are a long-time Secret Keeper Girl who has been to a live event. Maybe you have already read "Secret Keeper" and been on eight great dates with your Momma! Regardless, you, sweet girl, are a Secret Keeper Girl because you are a masterpiece created by God's hand.

SecretKeeperGIRL.com

Like us on Facebook!
Follow us on Twitter!

52 THINGS DAUGHTERS NEED FROM THEIR DADS

What Fathers Can Do to Build a Lasting Relationship
Jay Payleitner

Jay Payleitner has given valuable, man-friendly advice to thousands of dads in his bestselling *52 Things Kids Need from a Dad.* Now Jay guides you into what may be unexplored territory—*girl land*—and gives you ways to...

- date your daughter
- be on the lookout for "hero moments" and make lasting memories
- protect her from eating disorders and other cultural curses
- scare off the scoundrels and welcome the young men who might be worthy
- give your daughter a positive view of men

Jay will help you feel encouraged with 52 creative ideas to give you confidence in relating to your precious daughter...ways to hold her close and let her go at the same time...ways that will help her blossom into the woman God has designed her to be.

52 THINGS KIDS NEED FROM A MOM

What Mothers Can Do to Make a Lifelong Difference
Angela Thomas

Angela Thomas, bestselling author and mother of four, draws on personal experience and biblical principles to help you raise healthy, responsible children and establish strong family ties. These practical, quick-to-read chapters cover childhood through the teen years and are packed with specifics to help you...

- establish a positive, wholesome atmosphere at home
- make your children feel loved and secure
- teach and encourage communication
- know when and how to correct behavior and set consequences
- help your kids persevere and succeed

52 Things Kids Need from a Mom will help you discover God's wisdom for moms in a way that's upbeat and guilt-free!